A Life of Bliss

A Journey into the Heart of Creation

By Amanda McGregor

ISBN:978-0-9934881-0-8

Dedicated to my beloved, family and friends whom have walked with me.

The Tree of Life - Including the ten Sephirot of wisdom, understanding, severity, clarity, beauty, surrender, grace, foundation, victory, eternity - Painting by Amanda McGregor

Preface

By asking both hemispheres of the brain to sit back so that the soul can listen and process, you will find A Life of Bliss deeply effective. The remedy of an ordered mind and soul has much value in supporting us through the hurdles of life, so we may in time create our destiny. A Life of Bliss has a curative power of allowing sacred space of inner peace through understanding, growth in expansion, light living, creative expression, development, worldly relationship and global communications.

Written after working one to one with 4,500 people, A Life of Bliss is a thesis of living in happiness and freedom with very valuable experience guiding all thoughts and dictations.

Amanda McGregor has a background as an artist, she evolved the potential in using curating in development by embodying philosophy, spirituality, holistic thinking, through using creative communications and psychology. She has helped thousands of people, whilst exhibiting widely and allowing her creative freedom to be shared with a deep understanding of the soul, body and mind.

Her holistic approach helps intuitive's, creatives, businesses and entrepreneurs in development and communications.

A Life of Bliss harnesses intuition, development, energy, tantra and communication skills to help with inspiration, communication, development and entrepreneurism.

The author of this book is not giving medical advice or prescription treatment or dispensing treatment for physical, emotional or medical problems, please consult the advice of a physician directly or indirectly. The intention of the author is to offer curative understanding in your journey of development, spiritual and emotional well being. If you are influenced by the information in this book and decide to practice the arts described, which is your constitutional right, the author and the publisher assume no responsibility for your actions or consequences to your activities.

Introduction: A Journey into Creation

Stepping in to the power of our own creation is a journey in to the inner realms of the self, through a confrontation with the true self, stripped away and naked in both power and vulnerability. Internally we can seek the answers to questions accessing a divine understanding or philosophy, enabling the cogwheels of creation: creative thinking, communications and the nature of collective consciousness and union to find omnipresence and omniscience: extra sensory perception in clarity. The clarity we invite in allows directions and communications externally to find extra-ordinary levels of high performance, manifestation, alignment and symmetry with the world.

All forms of creativity are found in communication. Connecting to an individual to an audience, through creative communications and appropriate language is an art in intimacy, involvement, engagement, relaxation, empathy and direct communication. Understanding the mechanics of how to connect and communicate can be a lifelong journey of understanding. Some start young, as for some, creative communication is a question of survival: for others creativity is a colourful expression of vitality: a freedom of verse to enable dynamics to express through a flowing river of thought that takes them on a journey beyond comfort zones and limit. This in turn creates and allows an expansion of intelligence, communication and collaboration in co-creation. Most people feed off some form of creative outlet to enable them to feel nourished, understood and enlightened.

Everyone has a creative centre to resource their inspiration, depending on their values, lifestyle and experiences. For me the image of the heart of creation is the same as my vision of God's garden. The landscape is sunny and green, full of waterfalls, lilies; abundant with flowers and nature. Clear and clean rivers I can dive into, enabling a freedom of spirit and intimacy in which I know I am loved unconditionally. When I centre myself here, I feel secure and safe, as if on a mindless adventure; blissfully living freely in flight, with an open spirit. With a part of me there I can comfortably carry out my connection and communication with people and the world. I go to this vision often and bathe in the healing waters of the river to let go of my emotional debris and to restore myself;

baptised and nourished I am ready for the day ahead. I realised over the years that a lot of my hurdles in life and my professional aims were transcended through positioning myself in light or creating lightness. Lightness could be created through humour, treading lightly, feeling inspired, detached, giving energy to situations, others or myself. I realised the nature of situations changed through a centred path of blissful living. I actually resolved most problems and inspired most professional outcomes when my energies were uplifted and my sense of living in the flow seemed to accelerate. I realised if I could trust in the natural order of things I could work with sourcing my needs, manifesting my visions and enabling my projects to deliver. If I could trust in the natural internal order of things, I was able to enjoy a sense of resolution and freedom. This liberty required some work though, as the world presented challenging processes; I realised the financial system, the medical system, the legal system, the education system were ordered in a way that was against the benevolence of the majority of persons, mainly due to commercialism.

I went through a process of unravelling the findings and dealing with the issues that presented in an extremely tiring and arduous journey of my twenties. I went on to work as a consultant, therapist and psychic in Covent Garden and near Bond Street in London. Here I was able share my learning, intuitive skills and development options with thousands of persons, giving 4,500 appointments. Seeing so many taught me many aspects about divine ordering; dealing with life and living through one's self created bliss. I realised bringing awareness to these findings enabled people to come in to their power; to step out of their oppression, pain, insecurity, depression, anxiety, sense of belittlement and limit; I found I could help to set people free.

To create an ordered 'omnipresence' we must understand a little about the philosophy of creation. We also need know how to work with our natural technology. We first need to look at the dynamics of creation and our attainment to nature. What enables us to feel we are creative?

I started to enhance my creativity from the age of six. There were aspects of my childhood which were very stressful and painful, I discovered that the process of painting and creativity gave me a profound experience that took me away from my worries as I entered a peaceful, warm and blissful holding. When I was in my flow I was held by a strong energy, the experience gave me peace and nourishment and was to stay with me for my life. My first artistic painting was of some purple violets, I looked at the painting and was amazed to see the likeness of the flowers in my work, at six this inspired me, the magic was in the mimicking, in the ability to mirror a natural object in life; I accessed a profound feeling as if awakening to a much bigger understanding: universal understanding. The process of creativity helped me to experience an expanded reality, as if meditating on the universe. Although as a child I had no words to explain this phenomena, the understanding never left me, I found a calling in walking towards the 'understanding' of this process for the rest of my life.

At such a young age I decided I wanted to be an artist. I wanted to 'stand under' creation in more ways than art. I wanted to understand the consciousness of 'Creation'. As an adult, I went on do a B.A.(Hons) in Art and an M.A. in Curating Art, I then studied philosophy, psychology, consciousness and energy, becoming accredited as a 'Creative Development Therapist'. I realised the development of art history represented shifts in consciousness, the source of that inspiration expressed itself through different mark-makings and perceptions in historical creativity. I discovered that by tapping in to the different models of creative channel I was able to express myself with different styles and talents that mimicked much of the styles developed in art history.

When I was twenty one, I experienced a major illness, Myalgic Encephalomyelitis, commonly known as Chronic Fatigue Syndrome. In those days, most doctors did not understand the condition, yet I experienced temporary paralysis and on some days did not have the energy to even listen to a radio. I became a prisoner of my body. At 21 I spent two years in a traumatic state of confusion and loss. One year and a half in, I was desperate to unlock the illness. I had an idea that was due to change my life forever:

I played with the idea that if we there was any truth that we had a soul, through eternal life giving experience, my soul should be able to unlock my plight and find a way out of my situation. I suggested that my mind take a back seat from governing my body and I invited my soul to be the dominant governor of my perception, awareness and well being. My mind's eye took a back seat in my head and allowed the expansion of my soul to rise. In doing this I did unlock my illness, in a phenomenal way. In one month my entire experience of reality shifted and I started to attune to energy, universal consciousness and I did recover. I unlocked my spiritual identity, I became acutely aware of the spiritual world, angels, energy, consciousness, God, even demons. This was a very hard transition, as I moved philosophically from a place of radical doubt in to the light, as Socrates explains; from the cave into the light. I anchored my perception around truth. My body went through what I now know as a kundalini awakening; I had soul memories from Egyptian times. When a priest came of age then, they were initiated in to their power, they were often entombed with a threat, like snakes or crocodiles to catalyse their spiritual perception, power and enlightenment. They were then asked to visit the four corners of Egypt through astral travel. As I started to explore my new skills I became aware that my ability with remote viewing, was profoundly accurate.

At such a young age, the significance, achievement or weight of this experience was not seen by anyone around me. I was undermined and asked to fit in to mainstream activity and perception. However, fitting in to mainstream perception, over time became a very difficult task, eventually I broke away from these projections and the sense of belittlement, finding my own path in research and development, until I was able to integrate and communicate from a place of trust. I went on to work in central London, Covent Garden, where I offered a drop in service of psychic or intuitive healing and development. I saw thousands of people, realising that life impacts us in very different ways but the structure of our soul is very much the same, therefore our healing can be remedied through an understanding of our soul anatomy.

I became a navigator of my soul, my own internal communications and learnt to express myself creatively through a highly articulate form of communication that worked both in my internal system, my inner voice and as an outer expression for art, business and global communications.

Over the years those skills have naturally evolved and developed giving me clarity with a professional understanding of creativity, development and communications. I help individuals, organisations, entrepreneurs and companies to excel. A Life of Bliss is written to enable those who already recognise they are on a unique journey in their life, in which they have noticed that their intuition fully serves them to make decisions and to nurture growth in their world. The book is a philosophical and psychological look into intuitive business, creativity and relationships, designed to enable high performance and constructive relationships and to help in all areas of life, allowing creative communication to lead to communion and an enhanced sense of community in global culture.

As I developed I realised that the efforts I was putting in to bridge mainstream understanding with others were not always needed or necessary to experience a sense of unity in collective understanding. However, in sustainable relationship an understanding and empathy was needed around the individual, their boundaries, needs and values. When in a relationship, we often find ourselves standing on two different bodies of ground with a need for a bridge in-between us. Meeting each other half way can sometimes be a complicated process. Instead of meeting them in the middle I started to use empathy. This powerful ability to stand in another's shoes, gave deep holistic understanding of the 'other' and peace. I found an ability to experience them in love, forgiveness, dependability, trust and understanding.

I developed awareness beyond the individual into a global understanding of development and international relationships, this started to bridge in to a global understanding of communion.

I sought to communicate the concept of the heart of creation and the flow of the energy of universal creation in a way that was accessible to everyone. Yet this was a complex experience to communicate. However, I found this profound creative and energetic holding space to be a shared place of consciousness. Many spiritual persons connect to the same energy though meditation and spiritual healing, many artists through creativity, yet I found one common experience that many adults could access without needing a creative, spiritual or enlightened experience, this was through the 'orgasm'. The orgasm holds us at the seat of our expansion and power, this enhancement of expanded awareness, high energy, white out, warm love and light enables a connection with all that is at Source, the heart of the universe or creation, through our senses; this is the 'Bliss Factor', the relationship to Source and a journey back to our origin. A restoring experience that allows expansion, unconditional love and a deep flow of energy. There are meditations to lead you to a stronger relationship with your sexual energy and 'source' as the book progresses.

The root word 'org' is about 'bridging'. 'Org' has historically evolved into other words around the concept of bridging; from root to tree, from branches to fruit, leading us to the tree of life. 'Org' has been bridging people through organism, organ, orgasm, leading to orgy, organisation: all as 'one', through out history. In this context the use of explaining orgasm through to an orgy is a symbolic reference to being one in lightness; in the experience of the warm and very light bliss of orgasm. This can be seen as a holding space, as if helping a person to experience the universe as the heart of creation. The sense of expansion connects us with a collective consciousness, a sense of oneness.

Connecting with the heart of creation is an individual understanding, one's understanding depends on one's experiences and relationships, however the expansion can be shared with a special connection with another. This connection seems to tap in to an abundance of source energy, the warm infinite sense of lightness that is beyond emotional complexity and physical reality, the centre of the experience is at 'Source', an abundance of peace, love and light that restores, nourishes and regenerates.

This 'holding space' can be nurtured through the use of high values: in unconditional love, non judgement and healthy boundaries, nurturing high energy and trust. To surrender into the lightness of bliss, we clear the elements that stop us collaborating: like fear, insecurity or pain, creatively expressing ourselves and allowing an intimate collaboration so we can act from a place of being 'one', life just is.

Using the spiritual value of simplicity, we can dedicate our energies of relationship to those whom we value and connect with. We can allow those who want to be bridged to come forward, to allow connection with those persons and with the Universal Energies, the connections just are.

We use unconditional love and non-judgement to create healthy and sacred space, allowing one on one intimacy in partnership. The freedom is in the allowance, to let go of bridges, to let go of wanting to reach, but to simply to be, to allow presence in, the presence of deep love and light, through a loving growth and nurture of blissful living and 'universal' understanding.

Organism₂ - An individual animal, plant, or single-celled life form; a living being. Oxford Dictionary

1 THE TRUE NATURE OF BEING HUMAN

In ancient times the mind was considered an organising tool, the logos, created logic in the mind in the principle of 'universal' thought and 'creation'. Logos, a Greek word, was achieved by attuning to the nature of the universe, giving harmony to man and God. The power of the word, speech and the principle of understanding was fully understood through 'logos', the divine order of creation, this was accessed through man finding his omnipresent and omniscient sense of reality. By ordering his internal thoughts and presence, he expressed that order externally through universal consciousness and the power of 'one'. A harmony and balance in the community has the potential to invite a communion of homeostasis: a community with profound balance and very sophisticated natural technology, that maybe only very ancient civilizations could have adhered to.

Being human is something we take for granted. If you are reading this you are likely to be human. However, how does our 'technology' beyond our anatomy and physiology really dictate our experience of human nature? To be able to explore the technology of human kind we need to go beyond the elements we already know and take for granted, re-defining our concept of being. Recognising those sensory perceptions that evolve through our experiences; in dream time, intuition, sensitivity, mindfulness, spirituality and expanded states of intelligence. Recognising the elements that help us to experience our own 'technology', helps us to see that we are highly advanced and very sophisticated organic human devices. However, in modern life it is very hard to find the way in to gaining control over these intelligence systems. We begin by identifying the nature of being human, by opening up the concept of our make up, inviting a journey into our senses and extra sensory perception.

True adj −

Conforming with reality or fact

Genuine, not pretended, insincere, or artificial

Showing loyalty to another person

Faithful to a cause, purpose, or religious belief

Conforming to a standard, measure or pattern

Conforming to the way things should be right

Measured in relation to geographic points on the earth's surface, rather than to points of magnetic attraction

Meeting the criteria for inclusion in a particular category, in contrast to being given the same name because of superficial resemblance to members of that category

Not relative as a value and corrected for all error factors, for example, the difference between true time and mean time; perfectly in tune

Nature n -

The physical world including all natural phenomena and living things

The forces and processes collectively that control phenomena of the physical world indcpendently of human violation or intervention, sometimes personified as a woman called 'Mother Nature'

The countryside or the environment in a condition relatively unaffected by human activity or as the home of living creatures other than human beings

A type or sort of thing

The intrinsic or essential character of somebody or something

Disposition or temperament in a person

The appearance or aspect of a person, place, or thing that is considered to reflect reality

A basic state of existence, untouched and uninfluenced by civilization

The natural and original condition of humankind as distinguished from a state of grace

The patterns of behavior or the moral standards that are considered to be universally found and recognised among human beings

The inherited genetic material that partly determines the behavior, character, and structure of an organism, as opposed to what is learned from the experience or the environment

Being adj -

The state of existing

Somebody's essential nature or character

A living thing, especially one conceived of as supernatural or not living on earth

A human individual

Human adj -

Relating to, involving, or typical of human beings

Composed of people

Showing kindness, compassion, or approachability

Having imperfections and weaknesses of a human being rather than a machine or divine being.

(ENCARTA – World English Dictionary, 2009)

Looking at the dictionary definition of the phrase, 'The True Nature of Being Human', we are able to ascertain that we as human beings are able to define ourselves through fully embracing our phenomena as individuals, living beings and inclusive to the collective in love and nature. 'Perception' is unique to the individual, truth is an individual phenomenon that does allow for us to have 'universal' understanding of each other. To find a way of thesis with the process of distinguishing one opinion from the next, whether it be through science, vision or equation, we can liken thoughts to logical thought patterns, 'concepts' of understanding.

A concept based around evidential information, is one element amongst a complexity of bonded elements, laid out in an infinity of wonder. So facts, as concepts even as proved through science, in actuality, can overlook and underestimate other factors within the duality of physicality, relativity, thought and perception. By trusting the system, the science of our humanity through the evidence we see, we may leave ourselves vulnerable to missing out other elements of influence, understanding, or the experiencing of other phenomena, other aspects of 'life' that as little evolved individuals, leave us all in a space of limited understanding. I am aware that no matter how conscious I become or how much scientific understanding I acquire in life I will always be humble to the greatness that the universe is.

The universe is vast, the genius mathematicians who endeavour to measure the greatness of the universe, can symbolise the vastness of space, unity, mass and volume through equations and digital apparatus but can we ever know what the vastness of the universe is like in our mind's eye? Can we ever experience in our logical heads the true perception of being amidst that 'vast' space? Is there an experiential aspect of 'nature' that takes us from the place of symbolic reference, logical understanding, to being in a position of understanding, a place of experiencing the true nature of the universe?

To intuitively 'know' something, is a feeling, a thought, a personal truth, a sense of peace in reaching a sense of completeness in which the mind can rest as all the facts are in place. So when we think we have an idea of how big the universe is because we are taught, because we see, do we have a feeling of it's greatness? Or do we just know? Because by feeding the mind in knowing, we may feed a limited perception, a belief system that has not got all the 'elements' of understanding needed in the right places to express the infinity and complexity of the vast-ness, in science, in spirituality, in life, in nature; all the facts at this stage in our evolution, simply are not in place.

However one thing we know for sure and we can trust is that everything is here; we know we are amongst the vastness of the universe. We know we are living in the infinite possibilities and probabilities that are, whether they be physical, spiritual, energetic, conscious, scientific, psychological, natural, dimensional, elemental and a bit of all, we are amongst the truth, we are the truth, even if we do not understand ourselves fully. So in fact to experience the true natural essence of being, we must 'be' fully present with all our senses and expansive states of being, in the world and in ourselves, feeling the experience in full presence.

Having achieved this state of clarity; in being able to 'feel' the 'true' essence of ourselves, nature and life, we are then in a position to guide our mind through the experience to a place of 'knowing' the true nature of 'being' in the magnificent universe.

Having perhaps found an agreeable position to begin from; in realising that the first step to awakening into full experience, is in being fully present with all our senses in the world, we have to look at that which may limit our abilities to 'be'. These 'toxic' aspects of life cloud our judgements and stop us having a deeply connected experience of life, infinity or eternity. They may come from social conformities, false systems of understanding, food chemicals that our bodies cannot process, from emotions, pain, insecurity, fear, jealousy, anger, resentment, deception, from threatening ways we 'perceive' the world to be;

all in which our bodies and minds struggle to process because of an inability to understand or to 'know' that which is real in the world.

Those aspects of ourselves and the world in which we struggle to understand or accept cause disassociation and disconnection from the natural world, ourselves and each other. They limit us in our infinite wonder, expansiveness and beauty. The limits stop us from allowing the universe to flow through us and touch all that is. The Bliss Factor is designed to bring awareness to the aspects that limit us so that we can step back into the magnificent state of full experience, enabling a universal connection with our omniscience, the technology of our humanity. The rewards for reaching this goal are expansion, happiness, understanding, life-purpose, well-being, freedom, light-ness, peace, love, natural beauty, bliss, expansive percep-tion, expanded intelligence, genius, immortality and the conscious experience of eternity. Imagine if life was so simple, that by using just two psychological and energetic elements; love and light, by centering with them, we are able to bring all of these gifts forward? I have explained that the lower emotional vibrations of energy such as anger, jealousy or resentment can block us from experi-encing life and connecting to the world but how, why and what can be done to have a more intimate experience of life, creating bliss and where does the creation of bliss lead us?

First of all we have to take into account all contributing factors in the experience of being human, even the ones that maybe out of our comfort zone.

Within my practice of healing structure, I work with the energy field of the human form, primarily accessed through the chakra's, the anatomy of the soul. I tune in to each chakra individually as if I were a radio using my hands as antennae and psychically or intuitively I bring forward energetic information in streams of intelligence, frequencies, visions, emotions, or I listen to streams of consciousness from a spiritual plane, God consciousness, or energetic frequency similar to tuning in to a radio through energetic consciousness. I then allow the energies, intelligence and scenarios to play out, to inform me and the persons I am reading for, in development, as if watching an animated life drama. This process, dissolves the lower vibration energies and allows transformation into the higher vibration energy of 'love' and 'light'. I have found the processes to be radically effective in creating change, well-being and in elevating a person's sense of happiness. 'A Life of Bliss' will help you to see, feel and experience the profound benefits of creating your reality from the two elements of love and light, taking us on a journey beyond physical vision, with an understanding of universal consciousness.

The journey of my learning inspired many gifts and an understanding of the components which allow creativity to turn into 'creation', leading to the output and delivery of ideas in the world as a part of global understanding, culture and integrated with popular awareness and communications, A Life of Bliss will share those understandings with you.

The areas I went on to understand when working with 'Creation' are as below. I start to address these questions from my learning and experience in Chapter 3, 'A journey in Consciousness':

- What is inspiration? How do we stay inspired?

- How do we remain open to the limitlessness of giving and receiving?

- How do we bring our future vision or dream into our presence?

- What is collective consciousness? How do we enhance global consciousness and access individual intuitive consciousness whist using collective consciousness for global communications?

- How do we work with spiritual intelligence, emotional intelligence, higher consciousness, heart consciousness, mindfulness? How do these intelligent systems collaborate together? How do we become human technological devices using our genius and creative intelligence?

- How does inner collaboration of our energies lead to outer global collaboration and communications?

- What kind of environment is needed to provide a stable platform for growth?

- How does an organisation stay as healthy as an individual living being or organism?

- How do we use the bliss of orgasm to reclaim our power in an organisation to enable co-creation or orgies? The bliss of creativity.

- How do we nourish and nurture bliss and plug in to diamond light energy resources?

- How do we keep a relationships and internal communications healthy and in collaboration in an intimate environment of growth and development?

- How do we remain away from the ego and attachments of power to surrender to the journey?

- Why do we use bliss, as enjoyed in orgasm, collective consciousness and lightness to reclaim our power in an organisation, or company, to enable co-creation and orgies?

- How do we remain in our presence in allowing spontaneity and intuitive procedures in whilst practicing mindfulness?

- The Ego, Religion and Spiritual Sexuality.

- Rebalancing the Energies of Masculine and Feminine.

- What is the Anatomy of Creation? If we are tapping in to our own resources, where do we look for resource and inspiration? How do these resources affect our creative expression?

- Asking the Right Question

- Sacred Relationship

- Using Intuition for Development and Communications in Business

- Oneness: Diamond Heart Energy

The one hand has surely worked throughout the universe —
Charles Darwin's Beagle's Diary p403, 1836

(altered in pencil from "I cannot think so")

2 UNBRIDGED

In the long history of humankind (and animal kind, too) those who learned to collaborate and improvise most effectively have prevailed. *Anon - (Many say these words are of Charles Darwin, origin of Species 1850 but no one seems to have found the source)*

Over the years I had developed many concepts around working with creation and co-creating, but I was struggling to define the right habitat for my needs. My attention took me to realising that a lot of my efforts were reliant on creating functional environments that allowed easy access for people to recreate and transform themselves through sourcing their own presence from their origin and initiating their projects and missions constructively, without interference and with dependable persons in collaboration.

I had realised that at Source, in our soul's infinity, as a seed of a human being, there were a few things we could rely on:

- That we were perfectly formed.

- That we were free of interference and corruption through others or from carrying pain, fear or insecurity.

- That the natural state of duality in relationship and in life replicated itself again and again through a deep connections with soul mates or persons that naturally mirror our state of being and experience.

As natural selection works solely by and for the good of each being, all corporeal and mental endowments will tend to progress towards perfection. *Charles Darwin The Origin of Species (1859 p491)*

I realised that the way forward into excellence was through sourcing presence at origin and allowing creativity to prosper. To enable these aspects we must hold our energy above fear, pain and insecurity, by allowing a strong platform of free thinking and performance.

I discovered also that to ensure healthy boundaries, and healthy platforms, our inner security needed to find alignment with the heart so that the future pathway is nurtured from a place of love rather than passion or reaching outside oneself for opportunity. Opportunity is a factor of the path; we naturally meet people who we can connect to as we stay in our flow, we catalyse relationships and allow opportunity in through collaboration, expansion and inspiration.

To be inspired we have to connect to people who genuinely are interesting and interested in our journey, so we feel connected, so we feel inspired or on the 'same page'. This shared understanding of values and pathways combines with a sense of trust in the movement of collective consciousness to operate within the bigger picture of Creation. As individuals we are all elements or cog wheels in those parts; all with missions, purpose, inspired creative channels and vessels of understanding.

However, to enable us to manifest and create from a position of our becoming or emergence we must take a future vision and work with it in the present. This process can create a problem when we ask, "Are we in the present or the future?" In the present we have to assess if we have the foundations to begin creating. Normally we question certain attributes to stability on a personal level. Judging ourselves and our assets we ask; do we have self belief, investment monies, a stable home; a stable relationship; do we have pathways or outlets for products or our created materials?

However, often the answer is in the pathway not the environment, so we need to look within. By letting go of our external environmental needs we start to trust our inner journey. This is an enabler in allowing our emergence or our ideas to blossom. Trusting our inner journey allows us to expand, grow and become a strong and powerful presence in the world.

Often we are aware of the people in our network. We can see our past and we can see avenues of growth for us to become active in particular ways of growth but how do we align the future to be a present reality without stepping out of the present and by ensuring we have the right foundations for growth?

We seed ourselves, internally and externally. We look at the elements of our value, the elements of our design; we look at the opportunities of 'spreading our seeds' and ways we can collaborate or catalyse others and other environments; we communicate the possibilities, the vision and the growth plan. We hope our seeds, once given to others, form a sense of cohesive understanding and we allow the ideas to incubate, to fertilise and progress. We look at the different techniques of spawning through communications of all different types: from meetings to social media, to pathways, to channels, to writing, to engaging projects and disciplines and we see which seeds are growing, which have planted strong roots. We look for a sense of uplift, growth, movement, journey, and pathway. After a period of time, we then go through a process of editing out or weeding the ones that are not taking, that are not sustainable, that may be flawed in relationship, environment, finance, cross pollination and journey, we nourish and celebrate the areas that are blossoming.

We focus in on the growth patterns that enable us to live in the now and carry on growing and expanding. The expansion we experience, is effective in all ways - environment, skills, products, creativity, lifestyle, travel and energy. We find we need a new housing, a new habitat to enable a new foundation or platform, for further prospects, we look for grounding. We go through an end phase, that is like the death of the first development phase, represented in closure, ending, death. We then re-awake in a new world of openness, opportunity and expansion in which we have crashed through new gateways, risen up above our hurdles to a new foundation of opportunity.

By now, we have identified the working programme or environment that works for us. We now know what we want and what we want to achieve. We have arrived in our presence and our ready for our future to emerge in the moment. So we re-package ourselves, our product, our services, that we have created, those planted seeds now fully grown and bearing fruit, fully ready for picking and ingesting; we are enabling the consuming of creation. We allow the desires, needs and wants of people to be met; we allow their vulnerabilities to speak in need, in seeking, in taking, in devouring. We speak to those parts that passionately love and connect.

But what are those vulnerable parts? We all have deep voids inside ourselves that we need to fill, to consume, to reach out of. We connect to the vulnerabilities in man, the ability to connect to other's pains are opportunities to connect, communicate or transform. This ability to connect to the emotional needs of people can be tempting and effective. However, we then relate in the shadow side of the possibilities, we are relating to the pain not the light. Connecting and empowering conscious man, from a place of mission, development, growth and love, we help to support and expand the development of potential. By trusting in perfect man, we connect in strength. How do we relate in lightness, instead of the shadow or duality of experience? We can start by forming loving and sustainable relationships based around light living and an exchange of giving and receiving or gifting, unconditional giving.

We allow ourselves and 'creation' to nurture, to nourish other's seeds, other's collaboration, other's love of light, beauty and phenomena in happiness, by offering the client, customer, collaborator, or consumer a sense of connection or space in gentleness, of presence and of love. We offer advantages; we allow philosophy to work with psychology, giving the advantage of an unconditional experience in relationship. The acknowledgement of development stages, helps with transitions and foundations of supported growth and expansion. Focusing on strong pathways we are able to source collaborative journeys, nurturing and nourishing inspiration. We acknowledge that human life is the facilitator, the channeller and the vessel in offering an intellectual pathway of creativity, of experience and a platform of light to enable an environment of beauty, strength, stability and consistency to take place. We allow people to experience life from the source of their origin without interruption, corruption or cause for concern. We enable survival to take a back seat and encourage knowledge to be shared and passed on. In doing this we allow consciousness to expand and technology to act as architecture to enable creation to consume information, consciousness and raise awareness in the development of man.

We start to realise that it's the process of the development of consciousness that enables creation to prosper, enabling the individual to sustain and life to expand and grow. As a collective we enter into the next phase of 'creation' .We become an architect for 'creation'. We act as a channel for inspiration to deliver on the nourishment and nurture of man; we allow man to flourish, to enter an elevated state of bliss, to expand and grow in a way that enables 'Creation' to show off it's vivid colours, perfume, sophisticated sensitivity in intelligence, technology and communications. We become 'highly defined' in the experience of inter-active communications and product development.

QUESTIONS ANSWERED

3 A JOURNEY OF CONSCIOUSNESS

1)   What is inspiration and how do we stay inspired?

Inspired thinking is recognised generally by a spark of thought that gives you an answer to a question put out to universal consciousness or collective consciousness. Becoming aware of the thought or concept, a person receives an uplift, a sense of light, a feeling of arrival and peace. Often, great ideas are benefited by many and may offer something 'new' to the present. They are therefore considered a new 'creation'. Inspiration enhances our growth as a human being, adding to our quality of experience of living.

To enable creativity, we need catalysts. Below are some tools for inspiration that help in creation.

- The communication of an unusual perspective, or a new object or artistic achievement.

- Access to the higher consciousness.

- A need for an answer to a problem.

- Living in a constant process of questioning with a dialogue of communication that extends out to the conscious universe.

- A financial need to create a product or service that can be enjoyed or is useful to a large market.

- An emotive need to create a product or service that can be enjoyed or is useful to a large market.

- A health need to create a product or service that can be enjoyed or is useful to a large market.

- Strong and connected relationships that enable collaborative banter, humour and discussion around topics in the search or development of pathways, concepts, or in enabling a level of inter-play to allow a light sense of creative language to enable creativity.

- A good connection with the collective consciousness, high energy, archangels, guides, or 'God' to enable inspired ideas or a vision; to have a 'dream' or goals.

2) How do we remain open to giving and receiving?

The development process of creativity to some level relies on a process of giving and receiving. That information may be inspired by development, nature, a person, or the collective conscious universe. In order to develop our processes we need to be able to give and receive in all ways.

In life, giving and receiving can only be unconditional when the act is healthy, when a person surrenders to the process; when a person's boundaries are respected or acknowledged; when the experience is activated from a loving and light position. To want to give, we have to be inspired by our own ideologies or another person, we may want to reach them, communicate to them, to share our perception. We may want to go on a journey, project or create an objective due to our sense of destiny, adventure, inspired learning or experience. When entering this process, we often unconsciously see or feel a future vision in which we hope we are investing in and maybe will be rewarded by a new avenue of experience, thought, ideology or understanding.

When we are bringing lightness to another's shadow, we may have a deep emotion in ourselves that we see another experiencing, like pain, hunger, lack, grief or illness. Inspired giving is about enlightening a situation, object or person. These forms of communication can transform and reward both ways. They work with light; these acts add beauty and respite to the world we live in and is a primary act or tool of creation.

Being able to reach another in an act of compassion, whilst being important to love and the serving of our community, also has a more self centred side to it. Compassion demands a sense of self-knowing, as by nature compassion gives validation and acknowledgement to our own pain, we therefore often feel compassionate in reaching another person that has had an experience we understand and know. We are inspired to give as the rewards include an act of self-love. Compassion is complex as this act of love is about connecting to pain, or trauma, an experience that happened over the line of healthy living. We connect in light; the act is delivered over another's threshold of healthy experience, which is often over a line of consistent health or well-being. The act of compassion often has areas of self-sacrifice to it's activity, so when one is compassionate, one has to know how to work within healthy boundaries, how to 'heal', receive support, supervision, to reward or grow from these acts of giving. Through healing and compassion both persons (the giver and the receiver) move into a sustainable place of loving nourishment and development, the journey helps them to expand, become open and trust their connection to the globe.

The act of giving and receiving enables the fundamental needs of a person to be met in collective conscious awareness; the flow of these needs being met enables a deep security which allows a lighter approach into development pathways. It is not until the fundamental needs of a person are met that they can move into a lighter sense of being, in creativity and development. We therefore need to resolve a trust with boundaries, energy and understanding about the nature of healthy experience in respect to understanding 'need'.

T o 'trust' in receiving, it is helpful to 'allow' energy, physical objects we need, or help to come our way; to come into our personal space by not judging the avenue of its arrival. This can be hard for some as there is a risk of being 'let down', disappointed or corrupted. Some people stay very much on the side of 'only giving', others in 'only receiving'. Hence the statement; is he/she a giver or a taker? We need to clear any defence that interferes with us feeling worthy of receiving in abundance, or knowing how to give freely and unconditionally. To enable this trust we can put in healthy boundaries, connect with people with similar values, check in with the care of ourselves, to rewards, tithe our income and affirm that we are grateful for consistently receiving from the abundant universe and the persons giving.

Healthy boundaries are recognised by working out how much you want to give before you may feel too much sacrifice. Giving can be small or large, checking in with empathy to the true nature of the person you are intending to give to, can help to assess a healthy and appropriate experience in giving. Recognising how your and their needs are taken care of, helps to assess boundaries. Boundaries, context and quantities can be communicated to give clarity to defining the nature of the gift.

Receiving well, is also about not taking advantage or exploiting a situation. Realising that if a person is vulnerable or very open, they may need help assessing the nature and quantity of what they are giving. Discussing the details when a person has regrets in giving and receiving and putting in boundaries, helps people keep in a positive position with giving and receiving. The person may have areas of interest that motivate and inspire them in giving in areas in which they find a chore or bring them down in low energy in giving due to sacrifice or compassion fatigue.

These acts of assessment allow a constant flow of possibility in giving, receiving, reward, inspiration. Allowing the flow of life to prosper and a sense of community to flourish.

We can always remain in a place of gratitude, to see the positivity in our life and work experience, being grateful for the aspects of life that give us something, even if not the 'whole' area of want. This helps us to see that we are being supported, maybe not always on our terms, but definitely in a way that is beneficial. Organising our life and relationship to people to allow more in, to enable life to flow in to a more expansive reality, does mean checking in with the nature of gifting (giving unconditionally), using empathy to understand a person and their needs and pains and remaining open to receiving people openly and with out judgement. Moving from compassion to empathy in serving others helps us sustain inspired giving.

Understanding from a place of authentic experience in the reality of another's needs, is important in true connections with collaborators and the wider network of persons. People can appear to be supportive but can be a little disconnected in 'hearing' the reality of what it is to be on a pathway or involved in an environment, or relationship. Understanding the true nature of a person's experiences, relationships, environment, brings authenticity into the relationship, allowing a 'real' assessment of understanding, trust and truth in the nature of living. By acting as if in another's shoes through the use of empathy we can find ways beyond control and defence; in trust, communication, understanding, nourishment and nurture.

Once the whole picture is understood, then it is possible to help. Active listening, means taking action in respect of hearing the person's need to move forward, their situation, pain, or area of problem, for real. If you cannot help or be present, then it is about assessing what else is possible. How can that person move into a realistically better situation? Ask yourself and them, what else is possible?

Assuming, judging, frustration or expectancy can create many problems. Giving support for the sake of support or advice for the sake of advice doesn't always help the person. Ask them what they need. How can they move forward? What is important for them? These questions help identify steps forward that support the person's sense of purpose and self-understanding of possibility.

We are then in a position to realistically find new direction, help, support, nurture and nourish. Help can be given in many different ways; through one's own inspiration, through catalysts of questions, through research, through practical solutions seeking to be present in a very grounded way. Listening and support isn't always enough, unless it is dependable to the help and presence needed in developing the situation on. Activating catalysts into new beginnings, pathways and practical solutions, can be achieved through real understanding, and active presence. Always ask, 'what do you really need?', 'what resources are there in your life?', 'which pathways can you activate?'.

To remain open to giving and in the flow of giving and receiving, we are have to be trusting in the flow of energy and other valuable areas of our being, like time, talent, finance, presence, love and relationship.

If we give on all levels to all types of person, we share ourselves fully and we remain open whilst in our power to fully being present with all our talents, which can be empowering. However, this can be detrimental to our own health through a form of self-sacrifice, especially if that which we are giving is not valued by the 'other' or carried out from an inspired place of love. We therefore can burn out and form a sense of fatigue, like compassion fatigue. We start to have a sense of giving ourselves away, through compromise, through closeting, through loss of energy, through others under valuing our gifts or efforts and we may start to notice we feel weak, or feel drained. It is helpful to value ourselves from a trusted position, which means a position in which we can sustain dependable relationship with others. People have to be able to understand our decisions, value us, relate to our wholeness and respect our needs. In a highly connected relationship, this is understood easily. However, when there is gaps of 'understanding' we have to be clear and sometimes communicate our needs with conditions, as if to express terms of operation. 'My terms are...' 'I can do (that) but from you I need....' If those terms are not met, there is often a breakdown in the relationship based on lack of trust. This means, time and reflection are needed. Clearly defining what you hope to gain out of the situation doesn't necessarily mean you will gain it. This is where contracts can come in. They can provide an anchor with expectations and achievements. When faced with a situation that makes you feel uncertain, putting down your hopes in writing and asking for feedback in respect can develop a map of expectations and begins a process of anchoring; a commitment into future objectives.

The mapping out process is done as a primary task at the beginning of the development process. By openly and clearly expressing each other's needs and desires, a picture is built up that enables the walls of the development phase to be understood; the walls of the vessels of creation.

If you find yourself in a position in which it is necessary to give unconditionally but you have noticed your needs or rewards or expectations are not being met, it is normal to end up withdrawing, as in this sharing there is a compromise. Sometimes it is important to recognise the smaller rewards of being involved but often a compromise is a compromise and as soon as you enter a sense of compromise you enter the sacrifice part of compassion. As soon as you feel you are self-sacrificing or you are beginning to give parts of yourself away, or you aren't actively receiving, the resistance kicks in as a non-sustainable or unhealthy way of carrying on. Resistance is formed from a noticing of self-sacrifice, intolerance or compromise. We need to be clear about the impact of these areas of sacrifice to ourself and in our communications, so they can be addressed or valued.

For the benevolence of all persons to be met in a family, team, group, in which relationships are formed through a collective consciousness, there can be times when a shift in the dynamics are formed. Often persons are resistant to allowing a re-structuring in, as there may be areas of self-sacrifice in that move. When the rewards of benevolence are for all, a greater sense of unity is enabled, other times there is sacrifice, too much is taken away. Resistance comes through a sense of sacrifice in going into the journey of union.

Questions to ask are-

- Will unity lead to benevolence; will this path be stronger for all persons?

- Will my sacrifices be met by rewards in other areas?

- What values can I express?

- What values will others express if I enter this pathway?

- What would it take to create benevolence for all persons?

- What options do I have in pathways forward?

- What am I inspired to give to this venture?

To help with looking after yourself, it is important to enable a safe platform of performance that enables a light way of interaction and communication in the world, a platform of light. Giving and receiving can get out of balance if there is a problem with 'self-care or self-love'. Being able to take care of one's own needs without too much self-sacrifice, healthy boundaries, or co-dependency is an art in sustainable living, in which you hold on to all of yourself and your power. Notice if you are giving your power away? Power is held through responsibility, understanding, vision, communications and direction.

Extending a tithing to other forms of value, like time, talent, energy, presence, we enable a sharing that extends our presence and allows a collective giving and receiving that belongs to a global consciousness and divine understanding. (For instance voluntary mentors in a specific skill set, charity, support or political development).

Learning to trust yours and others selfishness as acts of loving the self, designed to bring happiness to the greater whole can help come into a flow of love and understanding. This means removing the judgement of 'selfishness' to a place of understanding in self-love. This definition allows a taking care of life that gives permission for care and nourishment of the self. The catalysts of losing trust in others are around misunderstandings of boundaries, a lack of dependability, normally due to multiple responsibilities or ambition that ends up becoming co-dependent on others. All responsibilities have to be managed in a way that all person's needs, pathways forward and feelings are actively met. If not, on a personal level one may feel taken advantage of, not heard, trodden on, ignored or avoided. Asserting ones feelings, boundaries and the level of impact in experience due to the surrounding person's objectives can help to bring understanding, respect and deal with the nature of the problems. Sometimes withdrawing is necessary. Processing takes time and a compassionate approach to raising awareness can only be realised if the other people involved want to develop their awareness and the way they relate to you.

The allowing of the ego to 'take care' of itself in times of need or regeneration allows the individual to reconnect with the collective at a later date, the process allows an integration and emergence of collectivity in trust; by allowing the trust in, we allow the collective to be in a state of oneness. However, sometimes, the need to reconnect with the self to attend to those aspects at core that need attention, means there is a removal from the whole and others which can be contradictory to another's needs. Trusting the longer term process of change and rebalance, allows a reconnection in through time, after adjustment. So it's very important to not judge selfishness as one doesn't know the components of it. In time it is possible to allow the collective to re-group or reconnect, if that is what is wanted, but sometimes through allowing a disconnection we accept a deeper purpose in that space. Compassion to another is only effective if wanted for true and real reasons of equality, emergence, union and integration. Use empathy to understand the limits and possibilities of the relationship.

Those who 'feed' off others energetically without a conscious regard of other's benefits, wants or needs, or understanding around 'inspired' giving and receiving are often known as energy vampires. They need others to create their objectives in a way that makes others vulnerable to projected limit, closeting, undermining, insecurity and disempowerment. In this case the relationship is not active in its positively person-centred development or trusted exchange of energy, which means that 'others' feelings and needs are over-run for the benefit or advantage of the person taking.

Inspired giving arises when there is a feeling that you have the energy to give and a deep connection to the pathway of the experience, object, project or the 'other'. You may feel you want to help or share in the experience, there is an interest in the learning or an emotive, or the experience serves on another level. If a person, company or organisation takes energy from its employees when they are not connected to the experience, when they aren't inspired by the direction or work, they can run low in energy and performance levels can deteriorate. They then enter into resistance through too much self-sacrifice. People have to remain in their 'flow' and sense of freedom of spirit to enable a freedom of movement, creativity and productivity. Always ask, is the person you are relating to, 'able to serve my best interests? Am I able to help/serve them? Am I able to gift unconditionally?', 'Am I able to receive unconditionally?' If there are conditional terms, you need to specify, 'My terms are…' If they cannot be met, it's time to very gently find new direction. What are my options for new direction? What pathways can I explore? What is the likely outcome? Giving and receiving unconditionally is the positive place to be as you are in the surrender of the experience and the trust of it. Nurturing a safe environment that enables trust and

dependability, allows people to give freely and unconditionally.

If the relationship is very complicated, in that you may
sometimes feel boundaries aren't respected, occasionally
you may feel undermined or manipulated, let down or
disappointed and you really don't know if you can carry
on with the person , it may be helpful to identify the
nature of those experiences and trigger phases to bring
clarity. After a big 'let down' experience, we usually take
some time to reflect, we may lose some trust, or spend
time alone or withdrawn. We look at the situation, we
procrastinate, and we look at the nature of the area of
conflict in values, boundaries, sense of dynamic. We ask
ourselves, what happened?

'Bring Clarity to Let Down'

- What was their expectation?

- What was their reality of our experience?

- How did they benefit?

- How did this help them to move forward?

- What was my expectation, my vision of experience?

- What was my benefit?

- What was my reality in experience?

- How was I trying to move forward?

- What did I want to achieve?

- How did I feel afterwards?

- What options do I have for moving forward?

- What have I learnt from this experience?

- What values do I like to operate with when engaging with and creating these experiences?

- How can I express these values to them?

- What are my options in moving forward?

These lines of questions are designed to help us see the bigger picture of how two or more people's needs and wants came into conflict. To resolve conflict we need to look at values and reality of experience. Values inform boundaries and expectations in experience. When the boundaries of our values are crossed, the values are not adhered to, so there is a crash in confidence and loss of trust.

Different values that people like to work with in a relationship or collaboration are: Shared vision, unity, integrity, common ideas, 'active' interest, allowance, consideration, creative development, equality, shared benefits, rewards, common goals, responsibility on impact, after care, feedback meetings, team work, long term benefits, development strategy, long term vision, sustainable security, honour, empowerment, learning etc.

There are certain people in our lives to whom we realise the reality of relating gives the sensation of a question; is the glass half full or half empty? These persons we find we need to reflect on; do we love them unconditionally? Does the let down of their inability to be dependable mean that we carry a constant sensation of pain?

We can find a place of understanding through resistance. Resistance is about the inability to surrender into the bliss; love, light, or oneness, or to let go and fully be with the person you are relating to, we hold back. The distrust can arise from many different factors, including limiting beliefs, self-doubt, questions around the future, responsibilities, intolerances, co-dependency and lack of acceptance.

In allowing a relationship to grow, whatever the nature of the relationship, we have to fully 'trust' the journey and give ourselves fully, empathy helps us understand the other's nature and the risks involved in that surrender. Some relationships just need time to deal with the elements that come up that create limit. However sometimes problems arise that need to be dealt with; sometimes the relationship cannot move forward until these elements have been processed and cleared. When a relationship feels stuck, whether it be work or personal, it can be very de-stabilising and can cause insecurity and anxiety for one or another person. Areas of judgement, reward or need start to creep in and the process becomes a bit of a balance sheet around who has given what to whom. When a relationship becomes measurable it has lost the trust and is in a state of resistance. Moving through resistance is very difficult, because the process leans on conflict resolution and 'active' processes of change, to enable dependability, an opening up or a new beginning. Within intimate relationship it is possible to take away our defense around each other by reducing Armour, this can be done through talking and taking our clothing off, until ones heart and soul lies bear to each other and the trust is found in vulnerability, understanding, empathy and needs. Trusting in love and giving energy to each other as complications arise can help to avoid separation. With work relationships and friendships, agreeing to reduce defence systems, using different approaches in empathy, does help to bring conflict resolution. There are ways of using empathy in the chapter, 'The Anatomy of Creation'.

Separation

Often the relationship closes because there is a sense of 'no way forward'; the two persons may want different pathways or different outcomes. There is no way of controlling this phenomena, it is a process of life, in which some persons you will find walk a similar path for longer or are more deeply connected than others. When the relationship closes in and nothing can be done to actively change things, an exit strategy is needed. Exiting the sense of entrapment is hard and needs understanding to enable a positive pathway within it. To create positive exit strategies:

- Allow routines in, to enable a sense of reliability in expectation.

- Give spaces of time in which questions are not asked about movements or what the other is doing.

- Allow in the possibility of creating small spaces of trust to do with dependable time frames, agreement on tasks, allowing different choices, pathways and hobbies to have time.

- Stick to boundaries and expectations around timing.

- Use the above for helping children to find consistency and to be met with dependability and expectations.

- Consider using financial advisors, financial consultants, councillors and mediators to deal with separation using a conscious approach that reduces the need for court hearings and large legal fights. Consider using a solicitor to anchor agreements, choosing values that reduce conflict.

- Close the door appropriately at the right time.

- Seek help if there is a need to affirm boundaries and to encourage the other person to keep to agreements.

- Keeping discussions to an acknowledgement of feelings and on a feeling level, using empathy. This helps to reduce attack, defence, judgement and projections.

Look at the direct and practical needs of yourself and the other person. Checking they can move forward and have the right support to do so, from a very real perspective that is realistic to their experience and their pathways forward, ask them what their options are for support, so that there is a feeling of constructive development out of the relationship. It can be helpful to follow up for a period of time.

Trying to create stability during separation encourages a more grounded approach. Finding constructive processes in all exit strategies, helps to reduce the sense of abandonment or the feeling of closure isn't too damaging or painful for the person. Trying to love a person from a distance in respect to their 'reality' or real experience of living, helps to maintain a space for change and separation.

When a relationship has lost trust, the choices, or possibilities become greatly reduced. We have to detach from expectation and a need for them to be a part of our life. When we function independently we are not threatened by another, it is only when we need them to behave in a certain way we start to control and manipulate. Letting go and surrendering to the way things are, allows us to pick up and move forward in a self contained way. Be careful to notice judgements, especially around values, agreeing to detach from judgement, projected need and focusing on understanding can help to create some grounding.

Healing Resistance in Relationship

Resistance is a normal factor of life. As I said, resistance is about the inability to surrender to the trust of each other and remain vulnerable as the journey of life unfolds. If a person does not want to walk on the same or similar path as you, or they are not able to accept all of you, or they are not able to trust in your love and light, you will experience resistance.

The problem with resistance is it can be painful, as one can feel isolated, controlled or not fully involved, often there is a feeling of projected limit and the reduction can feel belittling. One person can have more resistance than another. This can feel like a rejection, abandonment or lack of presence. The pain affects a person in many ways; there can be automatic reactive effects through impact of resistance, especially if the feelings touch on your emotional black holes or sore spots (more in chapter, 'The Sacred River of Truth'). You may protect in defence, your way of protection may be complex communication; passive or aggressive reactivity. We can never fully protect ourselves from the pain of resistance, we can only get to know the nature of resistance as the gaps between us and another. Allowing the perspective of seeing resistance for what it is enables us to send love to the pain, sense of oppression or limit so we don't end up in projections or arguments. We have to accept we are vulnerable and it is alright to remain vulnerable. We may procrastinate and feel anxiety, insecurity or a sense of being disempowered. The pain we experience is due to our limited sense of freedom. Being clear about resistance helps to develop clear communication pathways so we know what to communicate and bring awareness to. We can give blessings for 'seeing' someone and their stage of development or choose a different path, this can help the move forward.

Moving forward may feel daunting, it is sad to let go or detach but it is constructive to pathways in which we are met by those who are able to be present, love unconditionally and be open to the full acceptance of ourselves.

By allowing life to be an adventure in which we try to stay open, try to allow yourself to be vulnerable, to share openly, love wholly. We can begin to get a sense of our own inner security. We can remain peaceful, offering love and detaching gently, communicating openly, we do n o t 'need' to bridge the gaps, we simply need to be present in understanding, giving love, whilst using empathy to relate: allowing ourselves to be at different places on our journey of life.

Ask yourself, are my true needs being heard, seen and actively engaged with? Am I able to walk forward with this person and still be fully present and connected with them? Can I fully accept them? Can I open myself up to fully receiving them? Can I open myself up to fully giving to them?'

What material elements do I have to let go of to unite with the other? Which responsibilities do we need to surrender to be able to actively move forward? How can I detach from the elements that hold me and tie me to this reality? How can we unite as one? How can the material develop or move forward into the next phase with this person?

When two people have a deep and real trust or allowance of each other, through active, real understanding and dependability in presence they allow life to flow through them. They enter into an 'honour' of each other and all persons involved. In the state of honour we find we can sustain being in light, surrender to bliss or happiness. We find our 'real' or 'authentic' life has a way of entering into honour through uplift, support, marriage, promotion or an elevated or enhanced experience.

Meditation - Claiming back the full heart space after a period of resistance in a relationship.

Allow your focus to turn inwards and concentrate on your breathing, visualise your breath as white light. With every breath draw oxygen in, visualising light filling your body up, as the light oxygen moves from your lungs into your blood stream. in time open your heart to allow love to pour through you allowing the love to spill out. Allowing your focus to gently and slowly move towards your heart space, taking deep breaths in expanding the heart and allowing the energy centre to rise, remembering the feeling of an open heart and the sensation of love flowing out of you. Reconnecting with the sensation of bliss or falling in love, remembering the heart fully open with an uncontrollable outpouring of love. As you feel this sensation allow yourself to bathe in the white waters of your love-bath, allowing a trusted and blissful sensation of immersion as you visualise yourself gently drifting into the depths of your loving energy, allowing that energy to grow and expand with every breath, enabling the love to pour all around you and elevate you, so you feel absorbed in the warmth and expanded state of being. As you go back to the circular energy of an open heart, visualise yourself standing at the edge in abundance of love and look around, look for any shadows, senses of impact, a sense of weight, or people that have projected a sense of reducing or limit. There may be objects or persons towering over your heart space and a sense of limit in your ability to take back the open-hearted sense of abundance. Please ask the persons to step back and remove the objects, claiming back your heart space and your freedom of open-hearted bliss. Allowing in a sense of immersion and embodiment in an overflowing heart.

As you continue to do this, repeat, I am love, I am light, I surrender to the trust of love and light, repeating this again and again, until the energy moves up to connect with the Godhead consciousness and expands into the loving universe. I am love, I am light, I surrender to the trust of love and light. As the energy elevates and uplifts, you will start to notice the heart of God presenting himself. Allow any sense of doubt or interference to clear and any fears, or insecurities to dissolve. I trust in a loving God, I surrender to the union of the collective, I am one, I trust in oneness. I am love, I am light, I surrender to the trust of love and light. Keep going, allowing the energy to elevate, turn golden and expand into an imagined vision of the diamond grid, illuminating every part of you and your vision, recognising the love pouring out of you and trusting the experience of illumination.

If you are with anyone allow yourself to remain present with the flowing energy, bringing a sense of euphoria and presence in love, sharing the way the energy flows out and amongst you, unifying you and connecting with your energy centres, creating one breath of life and one heartbeat, bringing the same energy of bliss into the physical environment and nature, so as to uplift and bring warmth, nurture and a present abundance of heart to love and share.

3) How do we bring the future into our presence?

If the past is our present, is our future, we are living in multiple senses of reality at once, but to be fully present in a creative place of expansion and manifestation we need to let go of the future and the past so that we can share in the relationships and development of our present. We need to arrive in the now, fully awake in our power, in the knowing of who we are and what destiny or destination we are living.   The journey into our future is through expansion of our already talented selves. We can do this by remembering that at seed we already have all our components, as a flower or a tree does even when it is still a seed. If we are born with all our tools that lead us to our finality, we don't actually need to look outside ourselves. We need to trust that our true inner sense of universe and connection brings us our wisdom and intelligence and together with like-minded souls and other seedlings, all who hold power in themselves. We need to trust that our intuition is correct in guiding us to our future vision; we can then embody our dream in the present by surrendering to ourselves. We need to understand our own catalysts of 'inspiration' and how that relates to others, how that inspires them. Through this 'understanding' we build 'trust', this trust develops relationships that when in the pathways of destiny, we become dependable upon delivery. Dependable relationships that deliver on ideas and inspiration help us to form our future. Bringing our future into our presence is about sourcing our true design at origin and 'trusting' or 'allowing' ourselves to 'emerge' in full power or talent, by nourishing those talents at source, making sure we have completed our learning, fostered our abilities, so we are ready to share.

Sometimes our original 'idea' or vision is simply a bridge into the next doorway of opportunity, so adapting to the environment and relationships enables us to see which seeds in our creative dialogue work for us, however we still need to value our ideas and our creations. It is important we understand which people allow growth, nourishment and nurture, as these persons enable a sustainable outcome in collaboration and delivery on value of self, product or service.

We can package the value of our intellectual attributes in the development phases by assessing the financial curve and hurdles at each term. Through an understanding of rewards at market and the rewards that benefit from the inspired connection to the journey or the pathway with others, we can assess the monies relevant to stages and put together an I.P., intellectual property package which aims to put a value to our product. As we centre the future fruit in the knowledge and expectation of the seed we can evaluate the right market conditions and environments to nurture and nourish full growth, thereby proposing to investors the budget, needs and financial plan of the forthcoming phases of operation.

If creating an environment for a platform into the global market, it is important to understand the culture and migration of pathways of growth and fertilisation through investment strategy. Often the ideas have to be aligned to the international migration of monies, not a more local idea of 'territories'. This enables a more buoyant launch of product that may favourably sustain interest and sales over more time.

- What is the nature of my seed?

- Which environment suits its growth?

- Which resources can I use to fertilise, nourish and grow it?

- What kind of investment of energy can feed its expansion?

- What are the components of this investment energy? (time, presence, expertise, communications, pathways, money)

- How can these elements remain limitless and sustainable?

- How can distribution become expansive?

- What platforms of growth in the environment can help it prosper?

4) What is collective consciousness? How do we enhance global consciousness and access individual intuitive

consciousness whilst using collective consciousness for intelligence for global communications?

Collective consciousness is the binding factor of being ONE as a global community, academically understood through philosophy. Computer science, social science and communications are beginning to mirror this phenomenon through devices, intuitive access to communications and more sophisticated verbal and written communications. To access this consciousness as an individual we can embrace information and communication through using our senses and developing our extra sensory perception using intuition. We then have various outlets of expression into the universe or global community.

Computer technology leans heavily on intuitive thought now, mirroring human nature in sensory perception. We are in a position to evolve our extra sensory perception to be effective on a super power level. Products and devices such as the ipad, iphone, Apple Mac products, touch screens, smart phones, smart products - which plug in to the internet are all intuitive in their access and inter-activity. These devices enhance the 'power of intuition', to bring access and technical empowerment to enable us to connect to extended audiences, vision, empathy, wisdom and heart intelligence, allows us to 'feel' our way naturally through the navigation of these technological systems. The usage inspires strong communication platforms through social media, through people ('crowd' conscious) and through the understanding of 'profound' access to each other. We can align to our own natural technology by taking our senses seriously; enhancing our clairvoyance, clairaudience, clairsentience and our wisdom, smell, taste and empathy (all five senses).

By turning this understanding inwards, we allow ourselves to connect to our inner genius; we become 'devices', naturally capable of inspired thought that enables our 'genius' to create on a level of global thought and crowd communication or collective consciousness. When we use this in business we open up the development and communication systems to become profoundly active in performance. There are many ways of developing our senses, but attuning to our inner world of communication and the detail of our sensory experiences by actively listening to ourselves, enables us to begin the journey of evolving our super sensory powers.

Organ₃ - 1. Part of an organism which is self-contained and has specific vital function. A large musical instrument. (Concise Oxford Dictionary , 2011)

5) How do we work with spiritual intelligence, emotional intelligence, higher consciousness, heart consciousness, mindfulness? Why do these systems need to operate

together? How do we collaborate with our internal communication systems to become human technological devices of genius to activate creative intelligence?

Splitting up the different intelligence systems enables us to develop and expand on our 'technology', intelligence, intuition, empathy and understanding, creating limitless abilities in growth and development. Enabling trust, dependability and ensuring strong movements in enabling a delivery of objectives.

6) How do we recognise these systems?

Spiritual intelligence is understood through a strength created in light and love, it can be described through philosophy, as an expanded understanding of consciousness and energy. It unites us to the collective and helps us to relate from a position of collective understanding, allowing us to relate in benevolence and intuitive understanding, which takes us beyond the norm in 'knowing' into automatic reactions that serves our personal relationships, the company or organisation. Spiritual intelligence can be an inspiration to philosophy as there are areas of sensation and experience that are hard to demonstrate through philosophy or science, we can use a process of communication science and psychology to bind. There are areas of spiritual intelligence in which we experience wisdom, information, energy, supernatural phenomena, light beings, love and light that are very hard to prove from a scientific point of view but give a strong quality of experience in living, are evidential and create strong catalysts of change and transformation. Spiritual Intelligence is accessed through all forms of sensory perception, the heart and the higher consciousness. When we experience spiritual intelligence, or spirituality we often refer to the experience of communion as a conversation and experience of God. Spiritual intelligence is abstract, holding vision and audio components. Spiritual intelligence is often a creative experience, the primary components of which are love and light. This identifies it away from philosophy; however spiritual intelligence draws on philosophy as a foundation from which to create.

Non-violent communication means speaking from the heart. The process leans more to gentle words of wisdom that enable feelings to be expressed and assertive directions forward to be clarified. The abstract use of the term 'I feel', is gentle and loving, allowing a space for growth and development and a lighter more intuitive management style of communication, that is directive in asserting goals and boundaries and creating a clear consciousness around roles. This form of communication aims to be unanchored as it gives space for transformation and change.

Emotional intelligence is felt from the stomach area, two inches in front of the stomach. The emotional space is an area that needs to be in order for successful collaboration and the area in which the motivations around assertive communication and boundaries are assessed then delivered vocally through the heart and voice.

Emotions are layered. They can be experienced in a multi layered experience, which once completely acknowledged leaves the person in a state of peaceful 'Source' love. This skill takes time to develop. Pain, insecurity and fear, rarely belong to the person carrying the emotions, so can often be sent back to where they came or out to the universe. Breathing through the emotions by acknowledging them, one feeling at a time, then taking a deep breath, releasing the breath, letting go of the feeling on the out breath, then re-connecting to the emotion under the last layer of emotion, validating it and acknowledging it then breathing through it. This can be done consistently until peace is re-found.

In relationships, management and team work it is possible to identify over laps, projections and underlying agendas through intuitive procedures, that connect with spiritual intelligence and God consciousness.

Emotional bonding with others seems to hold answers. The feeling of deep understanding gives companionship and security, yet our strongest bonds with friends and colleagues are through our greatest pains that haven't found peace or clarity. We therefore need to be conscious of how we are expressing our compassion and how our pains are finding expression and relationship with others.

The journey unfolds to help us transform into a lighter experience of living, relationship and collaboration. We can inspire, grow, transform and elevate through those connections. Emotional bonding is a powerful way of connecting but we have to be aware that it is motivated through a knot of confusion held in the emotional centre, however the connections we have with others in this way normally bring healing.

Mindfulness, is about processing, limiting and controlling thoughts that enter the head, reducing ones head to a peaceful and empty state. Mindfulness is reached through a deep trust in the understanding of life. To get to this point, one has to practice a certain level of 'control' or management over the mind, logic, awareness and ego. By slowing down our thinking we become more productive as the priority issues are dealt with in a more focussed way with less sense of stress or pressure. This allows spiritual intelligence, emotional intelligence or the higher consciousness to support the intelligence system. The mind then forms a different use in it's purpose; using logic for strategy, objectives, financial planning. Remaining reasonably empty-headed in other working processes allows other intelligent processes to develop, inner communication systems to form and for the self to assess inner well being and environmental aspects to find grounding. The intelligent systems have to be able to work together in collaboration such as soul wisdom, emotional understanding and mindfulness. The five senses inform the intelligent system's communion with their environment.

A person can feel 'sick', from two senses being in conflict or too much pressure, this appears to be a form of motion sickness, experienced as nausea. Blocks of flow to some-one's emotional consciousness can also cause exhaustion, which is why it is important to allow a 'light' supportive environment and spirited energetic catalysts to inspire and to cushion emotional resistance. Building up trust in the environment, people and experience when facing complications in senses can help to slowly find inner balance. Resistance can easily be worked through with a number of tools including emotional freedom technique and the Sacred River of Truth. These are very accessible forms of healing. Energy such as Reiki, helps to restore inner balance through uplift, allowing a person to flow. A person's flow is very important in pacing and enabling a sense of free spirit in which living in the present is very effective in dealing with the now and the power of dedi-cated and focussed communication in development; inter-nally, with relationships and communications.

In an organisation to deal with the ego, a culture can be developed by letting go of hierarchical or undermining behaviour. It's about allowing an organisation to co-oper-ate and collaborate with simply an understanding of different roles without an experience of being made to feel belittled for poor performance or weaknesses. These should be dealt with through training or development, more present communication and empathy that steers the direction of the employee into their talents. The end game is to fully be able to trust everyone and everything and surrender to the pathway of consciousness, or global experience and communications. An ego rarely recognises loving words as a threat. Non-violent communication, talking from the heart, serves to lesson ego defence.

Collaboration is successful when the emotive is in order and at peace. Those who enjoy working towards a common goal are given support in enabling this journey to happen through the full honour of their roles, a clear understanding of expectations, processes in delivery with individual support and understanding to create dependability.

The higher consciousness connects us with our innate wisdom; the universal collective consciousness, the universe. We experience this as an infinite flow in the collective, we experience the profoundness of oneness. We use this to bring inspiration, creativity, design, comedy and sophisticated writing. The process of using our higher consciousness gives us direct access to our genius and is the real control seat of our power. Some can access their genius through their priority sense or other senses depending on whether they are more visual, audio or an empath. The higher consciousness gives access to universal intelligence for all; the area to focus on is about ten inches above the head. Sometimes we need to work with hypnotherapy or self-hypnosis, especially if the ego is too resistant to allow the surrender to trust in communion without a need for control over personal space.

7) How does the inner collaboration of our emotions, senses, wisdom, ideas and intellect, lead to outer collaboration of worldly connections, communications and collaboration? How do we create peacefully collaborative relations with others?

How we feel about others, our boundaries, our movements forward, our sense of platform, is all blueprinted in our emotional centre. The emotional space has to be clear and at peace with the persons, circumstance, environment, boundaries and relationships.

Clarity comes through understanding, personal emotional organisation, understanding of roles, objectives, other people's motivations, rewards, dealing with bullying, dealing with mismanagement, enabling empowerment, creating healthy platforms that enable productivity and empower success, so that nurture and nourishment remain consistent and sustainable.

Insecurity is often catalysed or projected from an external party, however an employee may carry 'weaker' platforms(inner security levels) and not be able to cope with heavy projections from others, so they would become anxious, stressed and highly insecure. An inner sense of falling may even start to prevail. The inner sensation of falling can lead to failure due to coping strategies of reaching out or 'clutching at straws' to try to reduce anxiety levels. This 'clutching' o r 'reaching out' creates an environment of failure and starts to reduce energy levels and to be deconstructive. A management strategy of development needs to be implemented very fast. Insecurities can be dealt with through communication, energy healing, management, emotional freedom technique and active listening. Enabling the strong alignment of inner collaboration is achieved through raising consciousness in all persons roles, motivations and boundaries. Through making sure physical platforms of security are appropriate and compliment a person's real experience and inner self, a person can develop on a level of nourishment and nurture, finding new grounding.

How we relate to others in the flow of development relies on trusted, dependable relationships. Trust is formed through understanding and dependability. If either of those elements appear challenged or compromised, we become anxious and insecure at allowing the development of change to encourage the pathways forward. A lot can be achieved by listening and understanding to another but often there are life situations that create priorities in another that can interfere with the possibilities of the relationship or project reaching full fruition. Project or relationship delivery relies on the visions and dreams being fully supported and the seeds of growth being nurtured in their full cycle. For the seeds of ideas to manifest they have to take a primary avenue of process. I am often asked to 'remote view' or intuitively look at collaborative partners to see how their strengths, values, talents and weaknesses will affect the outcome. Any problems that may emerge can often be dealt with through stress management, teaching communications of boundaries and feelings, visions and clearly identifying roles, limits, underlying objectives and personal objectives.

8) What kind of environment is needed to provide a stable platform for growth?

Our inner environments have to enable a sense of strength and security in feeling confident and able to expose ourselves through putting ourselves out there and remaining in our 'flow'. The main unresolved areas of concern are in the family-centred space of emotion, to do with abandonment, meddling, neglect, loss and abuse. These areas can cause lost soul parts which means the person has left parts of themselves in their past as they were not supported or able to continue a pathway for one reason or another in that moment, that problem then resides in them in the present.

They may get depressed or 'stuck in a rut' with those energy holes. Those parts tend to be in a state of 'resistance' in the present. The person can sink down and not be able to perform in a naturally confident position. Interference from remaining on our journey, in our flow, in a constructive way has to be dealt with through asserting boundaries. Often interference arises when innocent persons who do not understand the importance of 'being in the flow', interfere with the space needed to act intuitively and consistently, in a place of unfolding 'happening'. Nurturing the flow is one of the most important aspects of business development, as this leads to security, opportunity and manifestation. Elements that build into the flow are recognisable in how they add to platforms for growth. They are persons as well as environments and processes such as healing, meditation, exercise, inspired experience and engagement with those who fully understand the nature of your path.

From a healing perspective most insecurities, fears, pains, invasions and insecurities can be resolved through energy healing, therapy or personal development work. The energetic uplift develops us beyond the interference. In an organisation, a person may need to be physically placed in a 'position' of empowerment to enable their activities and role to be performed with support and executed with a streamline conscious. They will need to learn communication skills: non-violent and assertive communication to be clear to those around them of their needs and the directions they would like others to take. When developed it is possible to put in energy platforms within their inner environment. Presently, I use diamond light energy, as the vibration is strong and uplifts beyond fear, interference, insecurity and corruption. This uplift energy needs nurture and nourishment but initiating or drawing energy from an channelled energetic frequency that serves can help a person consume, nurture and receive nourishment from Source.

9) Keeping an organisation healthy, as if an individual organism.

The word org, derives from a root meaning of 'unbridged'. An 'object' is either considered separate to a greater whole like an 'organ' o r 'organism' or they are contained within a collective, like an 'organisation'. If we want to embrace collective conscious, globally we are striving to embrace the whole collective market, as one organisation, we thereby bridge in to oneness and embrace unabridged understanding or holistic thinking. We may be aiming at one market, or a few, in which case we accept that we are not bridging all, just a few.

To enable this form of intimate surrender to allow integration into the collective or oneness, we need to build up trust, reduce stress, reduce pressure, enable strong internal communications and build up positive energy. The build-up can be likened to a form of positive intimate engagement. A lot of creatives use the term, 'getting into bed', meaning becoming intimate through creativity, collaboration and through business. During the development phase we use a form of flirtatious creative sharing, entertainment or comedy to create a light banter. We communicate and create a buzz externally. Firstly through our collaborators, that is often expressed into the media to open integral communication platforms, in forums and social media platforms. We then build up the discussions around the content and identify the development of 'trends'. We make the experience 'desired', engaging and attractive with rewards. A person engaging with this experience surrenders to involvement when they feel secure, happy and in trust, when they feel fully uplifted in a sense of light and and in bliss.

So the build-up leads to an engaging experience with deep, intimate relationships and satisfying rewards. The state of intimacy may have been created through emotional understanding, entertainment, activity, creativity, humour or sharing through the giving of love, self-belief or support.

On an individual level take 'facebook', the social media platform. Facebook has allowed a public intimacy in which there can be an emotional closeness and bliss can be shared with presence on a global platform. The rewards are considerable; there is love when a person is lonely, emotional intimacy when feel disconnected, shared experience of adventure or journey when in need of free-spirited life or creative expression. The process enables one to gain resources and perspectives and intellectual stimulants when in debate with like-minded persons. There is also an empowering aspect of political freedom, through easy access to parties, to persons in power, to bring change and to pull together in union. A casual and personal relationship can build in to opinion, union or journey. All these rewards take place from a position of ease, joy and fun. For sure there is a learning curve in knowing the boundaries of how vulnerable you can be, how much information to share, how to be responsible when sharing information that is used in global markets. However, my point is that the platform operates in 'lightness', the process enables an uplifting in sharing life's moments of bliss. When communications are sophisticated, we experience a place of gentle and loving understanding that allows social science to express itself simply and easily.

So the need for platforms of light in organisations and companies that allow collaboration on all levels can gain the company many rewards. By working with platforms either internally with individuals or in a more expanded context: with teams, departments, the entire company, or globally enables a sense of oneness without separation. We therefore find it useful to enable intimacy to be shared without a need for defence or separation: this is to do with the loss of the ego. Trusting in intimacy is to know that boundaries in the self are understood, that relationship is empowering and that presence or purpose is fully supported with the foundations that enable growth, nourishment and nurture. The process allows space for choice, for connection or passive stillness. In an organisation this environment can be replicated by creating communal spaces to relax, chat, share, or quiet spaces for meditation, the care of the team, collaborators through neck and shoulder massages, support, stress release and energy healing. Peace can be gained through visibility of the horizon, an experience of nature or natural light, the wilderness, team work, yoga or empty- headed stress release.

To encourage open forums of communication, people find direction in coming forward, in being seen and heard. The margins of thought in an organisation count and can bridge into union, as long as they are heard. This can be achieved by having a social sharing space for the company, in the form of notice boards, company newspapers, social media platforms, intellectual debate, creative communication platforms, and communication days. However these exchanges of energy have to be acknowledged and taken seriously through integration and process yet they can make a big difference to the individuals wellbeing and the union of the organisation. The elements of healthy social science are relevant to boundary, presence and being heard. Appropriate behaviour when in serious discussion or meeting for business has to be anchored with emotional peace.

This safety enables people to expose the intimacy of emotional and intellectual connection within the company, enabling a natural place of development for innovative and creative minds. Physical intimacy is different, but de-sexualising employees only leads to some very painful and dis-empowered relationships. Trying to encourage employees to avoid sexual relationships is helpful until a person has a true heart connection with one of their co-workers, or collaborators, then it becomes complicated on all levels. A person by nature needs to follow their heart. The effect of a relationship going wrong can be harmful to the company or organisation and employees.

As the roots of sexuality express from the seat of a person's power in the way they express their inspiration, creativity, energy source and liberation I feel it is important to not to castrate.

I suggest the acknowledging of sexuality with an awareness or responsibility around accountability. Bringing awareness to the communicating of boundaries, needs and bringing attention to sexual exploitation or harassment can help change the culture into awareness of honour, value, inspiration, understanding and trust in sacred relationship. It is important persons are helped with emotional strains and stresses and given support in honouring each other, from a primary place of love, attraction and communication through deep connection. Supporting persons in a nurturing way that enables their sense of integrity, inspiration and honour, to give space to the energies of union. Recognising deeper energies that bring two people into connection from a place of soul, open heart and emotional understanding can enable peaceful communications, if they are fully developed in understanding the difference to self-advantageous ways of relating and loving. The enabling of 'understanding', in which persons are honoured for their connections and seen and heard in their wisdom brings deep security and safety to people. Holding space for people does not mean encouraging them to behave romantically at work, simply acknowledging them, asking for discretion and helping them to create healthy boundaries which are effective and acceptable, in which they are able to remain consistent and stable without effecting others, enables a flow and processes of personal support through development. Thereby we can enable personal crisis to be a resource of growth: A place of emotional connection, learning, inspiration, enlightenment and development rather than corruption and reactivity. Thereby the role of 'org'-asm into organisation has a bridging point rather than creating separate entities. Expressing values, creating codes and ethics to relationships at work and in personal life, as if developing a culture with shared learning and understanding and encouraging 'love' to flourish in the environment. This supports persons in honour and can enable trusted communications, the priority being love.

In an ideal world sex would be a way of honouring another in respect, a way of celebrating another. A women stays deeply connected to her experience and the person she has bonded with, a man is able to detach and re-connect, whilst still honouring his heart. An open hearted experience holds communication space and integrity. The depth of experience when truly making love allows an open heart to operate in a loving and blissful state, from an integral standing of shared union, respect and pathway. A person in love spreads a lot of light around their environment. This is a healthy state of being. Understanding the process of 'letting go' or detachment can help a person remain centred. The emotional connection and bond formed creates a need for the emotional intimacy to be honoured. It is therefore important to raise awareness around 'unconditional love' and communications without ego or defence, so relationships never become political or objective in power. Most people can be flexible to circumstance if they are honoured, if their feelings are heard, or if their boundaries are respected. If communication remains, the flow remains.

The surrendering to 'allowing' an organisation or company to live and breathe without heavy control, enables growth and an independent culture which in turn enables internal communications to prosper. A culture of dependable persons is formed. The awareness of living from the heart and emotional intelligences, diverts the attention away from the ego and the need to take power through undermining and exploitation. This in turn has the potential of earthing the person. The ego has to be acknowledged, in self-care and individual roles and experiences, however, the remembrances of the collective and the benevolence for the greater whole enables a surrendering and a union in the collective that attunes to a large market or global position.

When people's jobs or environments, internally or externally aren't threatened they are able to spend time bringing clarity to communicating their boundaries, and directions asserting their needs, gently and effectively. They are in a position to expand, grow and surrender to the company directors and direction. They are no longer governed, their growth is facilitated, and the company's growth and development is nurtured into state of flux.

People's boundaries around workspace, management and emotional breathing space are individual. We are complex beings in many ways, individual's are unique but our saving grace is that we are totally aligned to the collective. It is therefore possible to trust that whatever the collective seems to 'be going through' or experiencing, in understanding each other, in growth and development, is relevant to each individual that is present. So giving time to emotional development and support through acknowledging problems with overlaps in roles, working values, poor communications. Giving support to persons in their highly pressured roles, whilst acknowledging their needs in goals and objectives can make an environment highly functional.

Most people are not taught how to operate in 'non-violent communication' (talking through the heart) or how to keep grounded and in check with the ego, or how to work with team structures without ego or dominance. However the teachings can be very simply and accessibly administered. In the past the idea of lovingly and gently asking an employee how they 'feel' about one task or another was a foreign language, now it is a necessity, as it enables secure working practices that encourage delivery and dependability.

Emotions and thought patterns are layered. Breathing through the layers, processing relationships, feelings, questions around situations, letting go through breath, brings us back to Source, to peace, to love, to the infinite. Operating from Source gives us a resource of energy which means we can love continuously and unconditionally. This means all emotional and political problems can be resolved. The bonding factor of resolution creates further emotional connection, teamwork, love; it enables a life of bliss in.

A person must be aligned to their talents and ambitions to feel they are progressing and living their purpose. A very small percentage will actually be living their truth, so to enable a strong connection with working processes it is important to help the person find a sense of purpose and mission which gives a feeling of pathway based on obvious natural talents and gives deep rewards to them in growth and moving forward. This can be done by looking at values in work and relationship and identifying highest priority intentions in everyday life.

By listing the values of each sector of your life, you tend to see what is important to you, to be able to work out your mission. List 10 values for each of the below:

10) What values do I look for in my personal relationships? My working life? My creativity? How do I find inspiration?

Hidden talents can be recognised in abstract qualities, like humour, in keeping people in the loop, in highly articulate communication skills, in holding facts and figures, in public speaking, in attracting a lot of people, in motivating others, in creative communications, in intellectual process, in enabling 'fun' in the most boring of tasks, in 'enlightened entertainment', by connecting to people emotionally, by the journey of enlightened understanding or lightness we allow an uplift and enjoyment. Sometimes the bliss factor can be nurtured through social skills seen in environment that are not normally acknowledged. Sometimes the sense of freedom of spirit is seen in the mind and body and in an ability to tread lightly through the world.

Giving over to the 'Will of God' through the hearts and minds of the global public, can be achieved by giving choices on global access platforms, which means communicating, giving and receiving that is inspired through and by the collective, through the people. We are facilitators of creation. The platforms that suit this in the modern world are crowd funded, trading, or communication platforms that enable global operation around choice, inspired thought and a detached way of creating money through inspiration. The connection to the global consciousness 'allows' people to fully be inspired in their own choices and how they feel about giving. Think which global platforms inspire incentive and choice to bring projects, products forward and explore real ambition, unity and social achievement into the global market?

11) Why do we use the bliss factor, as enjoyed in orgasm, to reclaim our power in an 'organisation' or 'company' to enable co-creation and 'orgies'?

By embracing the bliss of creativity we allow our 'passions' to serve us, but com-passion is a complicated word as normally this level of service requires a level of self-sacrifice.

Often as creatives we must go through a healing process to enable our passion to be healthier by working with 'love' instead of desire or passion and by enabling strong communication structures and intimate collaboration procedures. The need for emotional bonding enables a familiarity that encourages a 'family' type of atmosphere akin to unconditional love. This open and alive sense of being accepted in all that one is, enables a freedom of spirit to uplift the mind and give wings to inspiration, enabling a strong and working connection with the higher consciousness. The higher consciousness accesses our genius and the universal body of consciousness. Supporting this system enables phenomenal levels of creative concepts to be born, benevolence, universal connection through communications and deep and compelling 'understandings' around science, social science and philosophy, enabling environments of persons, companies, organisations and worldly development to channel in a direction of peace, productivity and lightness. Bringing bliss into contemporary living: blissful living in work, culture and home life.

Living on a plane of success, open communication and intimate emotional relationship gives space for us to surrender in trust: we start to feel a sense of belonging and home normally reached through the ecstasy of orgasm. This surrender of our will through the breakdown of separation allows us to embody each other through full acceptance, to work with each other's ideas: we allow oneness in and each other in without power or ego getting in the way of healthy relationships. This intimate state of communication gives us power as a team, as it gives us a close relationship with the intimacy of 'creation'. We can allow our mind to open, our body to surrender, we become energised and we can 'let go' of mind filled clutter. We are at peace and fully present with a divine order of universal consciousness.

This understanding of the energy and creative energies of Creation gives us our 'power' as it is also about a sacred and honourable relationship with God (the heart of the universal body of consciousness).

If a couple honour each other through sacred relationship, they naturally mirror each other, the natural duality of man, mirrors the natural state of creation. To allow the information technology of sexuality to express itself, we become mirrors of Creation. By enabling sacred relationship and sacred sex, we allow the consumption of desire and lust. This is healthy when held in a place of love, honour, respect and growth.

People who go on to share the energies of love, in deep integrity, without control, attachment, ownership or possession, often form different types of non-traditional relationships. Identifying if the relationship serves from a true place of unconditional love and honour takes a dedicated look. Becoming aware of tantric energies enables a strong sense of pleasure, love and erotism in light; in the understanding of sharing, giving and receiving. Perception, with love in integrity and philosophy can bring a deep understanding of persons and one and another that can enable freedom.

Polyamorous (multiple) relationships are formed from honour and dependability, enabling a value of communication in openness and a shared understanding of how to be present one on one with quality of time. This is a skill suited to those who naturally have a polyamorous tendency, whom naturally form multiple relationships, there is an art in communication skills, integrity, allowing a freedom to share love, their bodies and pleasures in life with a sense of dedicated understanding, agreement, honour and authenticity. People have different ways, with communicating their feelings around boundaries, needs, nurture, intimacy and sacred sex. The process of polyamorous relationship is successful with dedicated listening, sexual agreements, boundaries, understanding, integrity and sharing.

Finding your twin flame, the person whom you feel you are mirrored as one in your being, seems to satisfy on all levels and creates a depth in monogamous relationship if the 'other' is fully available and present, creating a sense o f 'oneness' with the opposite gender or partner. This divine mirror gives very little room for doubt or question in relationship and is often described as a blissful sense of connection due to the profound experience of understanding, 'universal' experience and engagement on all levels.

Soul mates can come into our lives from many directions and for many reasons. Keeping an understanding of 'love' central to emotional and psychological growth, karmic unfolding, gives space for change and allows an unravelling of a journey and learning, in which pathways find direction, adventure and experience. Those that remember their past lives or find out their past lives, can tell which soul foundations their relationship is built on and which direction to take the healing process. These soul memories are very helpful in nurturing direction, management of karma and growth. Soul mate relationships last for as long as they serve. To bring healing to karma both parties have to want to serve each other in growth, change and transformation. New learning always comes through the connection but sometimes the level of dedication in healing is not met by both parties. Most people have soul mate relationships.

Beyond relationships we find ways of communicating and relating to the universe through nature. Simple and peaceful ways of nurturing creation and finding satisfaction in daily life include looking at the horizon whilst watching the sun going down, seeing innocence in the young, finding joy in human relationship, connecting with nature, creativity, music, gardening; loving and honest relationships with all things and beings that are natural.

This way of relating to creation with integrity allows creativity to speak through us; we are able to allow creation to be a channel in co-creation, we realise the universe is consciousness and relating to us in everything we are and everything we do. We become a collaborator of nature. We therefore need to see that creation's 'will' is more powerful to serve than our own will, in surrendering to the oneness of bliss we allow creation to channel through us and for us to celebrate creativity: we allow ourselves to become servants of creativity. Thereby we 'stand under creation'. We now 'under-stand' creation and the dynamics that serve us.

We have become the creators of creativity, creation flows through us. Enjoy allowing inspiration to guide, the passion and bliss to dictate. You are the master of your own limitless potential, you are as powerful and wise as the universe and as deep and intimately connected as the God consciousness as you allow. Love and you will be loved; all you create and produce will be replicated and sent out to the world repeatedly. You are connected and in 'communication' with all that is but use this skill wisely as to love, is to nurture and nourish.

The Ego, Religion and Spiritual Sexuality

We all have domineering aspects of ourselves that we hold onto and which we remain in trust with. These are the aspects of ourselves that function effectively and hold talent, so we may feel a need to protect them. The parts of our environment and ourselves that work for us, also tend to be the foundations of our success. They work to set us free and give us a positive sense of pathway in expansion and growth. However when in a relationship, those aspects that we are inclined to protect when forming intimacy can easily become exposed as re-activity. Having feelings for another magnifies our sense of emotion and tends to shine a light on the nature of the 'ego', the control over the environment, defence and the way the self projects a sense of expectation on another. The heart may defend to a level beyond the logical, sabotaging a sense of honour, respect and equality.

When we enter into a relationship, we have an understanding of our 'peace' and how to experience acceptance on a deep and expansive level. We need our prospective partner to present to us in an open and honest way, yet the nature of 'fear' and the need to protect the heart from pain, often means a more complex set of circumstances present.

To explain this I am going to use historical references to spirituality, crossing faith and community life. This is a big subject as the projection of the ego onto community becomes a complicated array of sexual expression and understanding of creation and consuming.

We start through an understanding of a rebellion against love. Why would we rebel against love? Although the sensation of being in love can be warm and protective, there is another side of love that can be painful, entrapping, confusing and consuming. The rebellion away from love is often encouraged by desire, the want for more, the need for a part of ourselves to be heard, to be expressed and to be understood. This may be sexual, emotional, intellectual or spiritual. However, we may not have tried to express our feelings around all those complications within our 'love' situation. Or we may have tried but an active response was not given. So the desire for more is invoked and a rebellion against the 'communion' of love inspired. This action is catalysed further when we take matters into our own hands away from the central loving power supply, the heart.

When in trust we allow our energies to enter a communion with the universe; we vibrate and pulse out messages to the universe in our needs and journey and we are met with a profound synergy, inspired by experience and vision, as people walk on our path and develop our purpose with us in alignment with us emotionally, physically and spiritually. We become everything we are meant to be, as our design is fully met with a connection spiritually, physically and emotionally. God loves, the universe loves, the universe is conscious to our needs and our destiny. We just need to be open to receiving, so understanding why we may have closed down is important.

Historically the path away from love into ego, is represented by Lucifer's story. Lucifer was originally recognised as an angel of the Lord, then as the morning star, said to shine at dawn and be a mark of light in daylight. When King Nebuchadnezzar II of Babylon(605 BC-562 BC) was in reign, he is said to have boasted to God. As a consequence, he is said to have become like an animal. There are many myths around this story suggesting the debauch of the following seven years and the implementing of the Towers of Babel (gateway to God). The towers of Babel were originally to be built on the plain of Shinar, as a build to bring people closer to God. Yet the king's head was getting full as he became too proud and individualistic, following his own desires and expressing his own projections of wealth. The towers of Babel are said to have not been built; as God intervened by sending multiple tongues and languages, to confuse people and to stop them being in communication with each other. This could be seen as a separation to the 'communion' with God and an intervention by God to attempt to express the problem of separating the self, moving towards the ego and building up one's desires into debauch. The reign of King Nebuchadnezzar II (605 BC-562 BC) was full of fortune until it went to this end.

During this time Lucifer was said to be depicted as Satan. There is the fall of him as the morning star or Lucifer into different entity, with a different name, Satan.

"How art thou fallen from heaven, O Lucifer, son of the morning! How art thou cut down to the ground, which didst weaken the nations! For thou hast said in thine heart, I will ascend into heaven, I will exalt my throne above the stars of God: I will sit also upon the mount of the congregation, in the sides of the north: I will ascend above the heights of the clouds; I will be like the most High." Isaiah 14:12-14

Satan is then said to have gone to the Garden of Eden and encouraged Eve to rebel against God.

'And when Eve saw that the tree was good for food and it was pleasant to the eyes and a tree to be desired to make one wise, she took of the fruit thereof and did eat and gave also unto her husband and he did eat.

And the eyes of them both were opened, and they knew that they were naked; and they sewed fig leaves together and made themselves aprons.'

Genesis 3 (King James Version)

The act of a move away from love is represented in religion in different ways. In Christianity, this move is represented by Adam and Eve and the Garden of Eden. The Garden of Eden for me is similar to my visions around the Sacred River of Truth, a place of abundance in nature, warmth, fertility, harmony and beauty. As we move away from our inner 'sacred' truth of love and the God head of love, we allow the illusion of a 'lesser' truth based on a material value or egoist perception or individualism to cloud our judgement and start to follow our heads instead o f 'divine will' or our hearts inspired by the God head. We thereby loose 'faith' not only in the collective, but in God, divine will and in destiny. So we start to take control in creating our reality from a place of desired outcome, personal will, instead of in trust in our mission and purpose from an inspired place. This element of separation is a form of 'resistance' or 'rebellion' to the trust and surrender of light and love from an inspired place of pure white light, love and bliss: the God head of love. On the ground, true light and love is experienced, through people's hearts, with unconditional love and no judgement.

Eve's actions are said to be the birth of female individualism, or feminism, in taking a stand in equality and desiring knowledge, in rebelling against dominance and power structures. The story depicts Eve taking leadership in making her own decisions in right or wrong and to search for wisdom from taking fruit from the tree of knowledge. This rebellion also is a stepping out, away from the act of submission in being governed by 'man', through plucking fruit from the tree of knowledge and tempting Adam from a dominant position. This is sometimes considered a bite into a self-sabotaging destiny in awakening. Seeing or knowing too much, man eventually punishes woman by wanting a submissive wife, one that will follow and live within his desired lifestyle. By Eve taking a lead she also moves away from a desire in man to have a submissive wife, she wants to assert her own voice and path.

However when the divine feminine connects with the divine masculine, the masculine who has learnt how to celebrate Eve's wisdom and to invest in her nature, the gateway to the Holy Grail is discovered, the birth of wisdom, the womb of creation, access to knowledge and a portal to the bliss of God. Man learns to support and protect the divine feminine by relating and connecting to her magic, wisdom, sexuality and talents. This communion can be seen as the gateway to God, re-igniting communion with God, bringing peace and harmony to the divine masculine and the divine feminine. The change of relationship from submission to empowerment enables a different architecture in relating.

Women then relearns the art of submission to dominance, she learns that both man and women can experience an exchange in roles and enjoy the celebration of each others talents; they learn to understand their personal dynamics and the fit they create in relating.

The tree of knowledge, Genesis, is particularly relevant to the divine female. The intuition of women brings clarity and wisdom when fully nurtured. This desire for more understanding and an expression of God through the female form can be represented in many different ways, especially dating back to Egyptology. Stories say that the forces of the devil are seen to come from the initiation into the Kundalini energies and wisdom. However the devil was not fully characterised until post Christ, so these initiation processes of Kundalini awakening, that derived from Egypt (and India) must have been seen as threatening to Christianity. The stories must have been written later than Egyptology. The Kundalini awakenings were often initiations in closed environments with threatening animals and a forced need to expand beyond a sense of personal limit, to help becoming and integrating with everything that is, the universal body of consciousness, the God head.

Eve is said to be deceived by the serpent, Adam followed her, and they joined Lucifer's rebellion of God and love by focussing on the Self. The serpent also represents the Kundalini energy, the search for energy, wisdom and power through enlightenment.

So here the idea of Satan is born and symbolised in the snake, demonising knowledge and truth, which is then represented by an allowance of individualist 'wild' behaviour in human desire and lust.

However if we look at the Kabbalah Tree of Life(image at the front of book) and the seven attributes of Sephirot, we see a very different and largely peaceful depiction, as the male and female energies find union and harmony.

We see that knowledge has its own place in growth and life. The values of understanding, severity, clarity, surrender, wisdom, grace, victory, eternity, foundation, beauty as depicted in the illustration in the painting at the beginning of the book, all have a life force and recognisable place in communications. We see the male and female energies holding each other in the process of divine flow as the communicative energies of life, work through a tree of life in circumstance and experience. We see how harmony through acceptance and an understanding of eternity, foundation and the elements of creation are fully understood and embraced. The serpent seems to bond creation through communication enabling communion.

Post A.D. we have Christ consciousness encouraging an understanding of the journey of separation from God. Christ gives us a final demonstration of his faith, through his physical death and reunion or deliverance to God through ascension. He submits to his belief in a loving God and the following of his mission. Jesus surrenders to himself in being crucified on the cross, even though fear does make him question himself. This sense of surrendering or submission to the 'dominant' or 'governing' power is an important understanding in stepping away from the ego, in relationship, in circumstance, with an understanding of pain in love and collective consciousness. Jesus remains open to love without fighting but in intense pain at the submission to his destiny, his mission, in deliverance to the light and loving God, the ultimate service of (sub)-mission.

We see many attempts at trying to integrate the consciousness of surrendering and releasing of ego or dominance, in witchcraft, magic, and sexuality over the centuries. A space historically and spiritually has been encouraged in which all behaviour in community life is accepted, especially in paganism, tantra and the craft. Those that relate to Lucifer, Shakti, Shiva or Pan share an interest may want to express a collective understanding of community and communion through consuming and accepting all of creation. In early Europe, practice encouraged the abstracting of emotional relationship, by encouraging anonymous sexual activity, through the wearing of masks, or through a raising of energy, through hallucinogenics, or trance. Persons of all ages and experience were encouraged to intimately consume each other and surrender to each other sexually through 'wild' gatherings in the wilderness especially at Sabbat or the Sabbath; for instance at the Samhain full moon. These activities may have included incest, inter-species sex and self-sacrifice. This to me is a complicated understanding, in which it is hard to resume trust.

The thought of giving one's sacred body to the 'collective' sexually, is hard for many of us to understand and accept. The thought of just anyone sexually consuming one's body: murderers, rapists, paedophiles, thieves seems chaotic, disempowering and painful. These gatherings were designed for sexual release, non judgement and to hold a space for 'transformation'. The intimacy of experience in sexual communion, during Sabbath, with a sacred ritual was meant to enable growth and healing through the full acceptance of all members of the community from a place of light, bliss, healing, intimacy and into union with an avoidance of emotional bonding. However, engaging in these kind of passionate activities meant there could also be a 'sacrifice' to the self, this could often be detrimental. There could be babies created through inter sexual relationships, corruption of personal relationships, complications around control, disempowerment, body sacrifice, torture, rape, disease; the list was endless. These activities seemed to represent 'man's' need for sexual freedom, to control his ability to ravage in sexual consumption freely, the community acted as 'one' body.

However if one is in the unfortunate position of already being assaulted, consumed, sacrificed without consent, against will. We can look back and see this happening as one off experiences over a life time. So that which we attract in from a collective can be magnified, expressed and 'seen', through one community event, in this case it was arranged and took place on the Sabbat. A semi-controlled environment in which the wild enabled diverse unrestricted encounters, the transcendence of radical life issues, karma and learning. The issues revealed where taken on and experienced as one.

The personal need for man to be fully accepted in his wild side, meant that there have been many initiations into cult activities to create circles for men and women to operate in their shadows without judgement. In modern day society there is a strong movement to accept man's 'wild' side. Many men have wild dreams and dark nights of the soul in which their desires express, often they do not tell anyone. In their dreams they may experience themselves murdering, raping or assaulting. Help and release is found through the creation of places for acceptance, transformation and healing through environments in which these aspects can be discussed, the emotions can be acknowledged, the pains can be aired, the energies can find their light or higher vibration, with practical, creative and safe ways to develop boundaries and expression to enable a lighter reality. Some more diverse erotica movements allow physical exploration of these emotions and issues.

At the open gatherings women often supported and enjoyed their own release and wild side, embracing the attention and the freedom. There is an exchange of support to 'man's' wilder behavior. Sexual activity in trance enabled the power of the universe to work through the collective, to enable transformation and profound understandings to reveal themselves. Giving oneself as a vessel of God in sacrifice meant the soul could step out of the body to enable sexual engagement. Women who supported transformation, or bought healing in temples or sacred spaces, when sexually engaged with the community were often later called Sacred Priestesses, they would work from temples or sacred 'houses'. The sacred prostitutes where often called 'The Whores of Babylon', these were the women that rode their passions or desires without self judgement. A Russian engraving from the 1800's symbolically depicts a women riding desire through a Sirrush. Alistair Crowley's lust card is very similar.

When polyamorous women or men support a man or women through a love triangle, an affair or an open relationsip in present times, as long as there is transparency and integrity there is less judgement. A triangle is a strong structure but often relies on all three persons to remain strong. Sometimes through the secondary partner there is space for change and for transformation. However with deception there is disempowerment and a betrayal of sexual agreements which leads to a loss of trust and often the breakdown of the relationships. All parties have to agree to the triangle or other party and see the benevolence of the experiences for them to work, this involves courage, inner-security and integrity.

Often the desire for freedom in physical expression outside the primary relationship, is acted on in a kind of naive innocence. The extreme interference on sacred love isn't fully understood or honoured, the tools for gaining 'more' out of the primary relationship, aren't sought out. Holding space in love and housing monogamous relationship, is an art within the architecture of companionship. Without a heart centre, the love can become corrupted and the interference on personal relationship, heart connection and dependability can become a major problem. The symbolic idea of 'devil' or a playground for 'Satan' to control, disempower, corrupt, entrap and consume away from love is very real. The breakdown of relationship when dependability goes, is very fast. The architecture of a changing environment in relationship is held with love as a primary value. Holding space with non-judgement, transparency, dependability, learning, growth and truth help to encourage a peaceful journey of change.

Relationships can be rebuilt through understanding, dependability and raised consciousness as long as all parties are in agreement to work together at recovery.

Historically, magick through sacrifice and sexual consuming of the Priestess occurred frequently, with the 'sacred female' giving herself to men, as the 'Holy Grail' of God's Creation. Her womb and cervix were a vessel for her juices which flowed in abundance representing the juice or blood of creation as her divine intuition and sacred understandings brought wisdom through as a channel for men to experience divine bliss in creation through orgasm. The menstruating woman was seen to have power in her blood, the blood shared and worshipped. Here we see the link to the Holy Grail as a chalice in Christianity, direct from the symbolism as the female being seen as the Holy Grail, with a move in androgyny of female to male patriarchy in the 'blood of Christ'. Christ was considered the image of God in male form. The priestess was the ultimate connector or gateway to God through sexual connection, invoking the divine energies that lead to orgasmic bliss. The priestess's sense of sacrifice was empowered and supported through her worship; she may have allowed multiple persons to sexually enjoy their journey into light, experiencing the energies of divinity and the sense of swollen vagina and bliss through orgasm and the sacred river of excreted juices.

For men and women - Initiating your inner pelvis into the blood of Christ, invoke the energies of Christ in your pelvis;

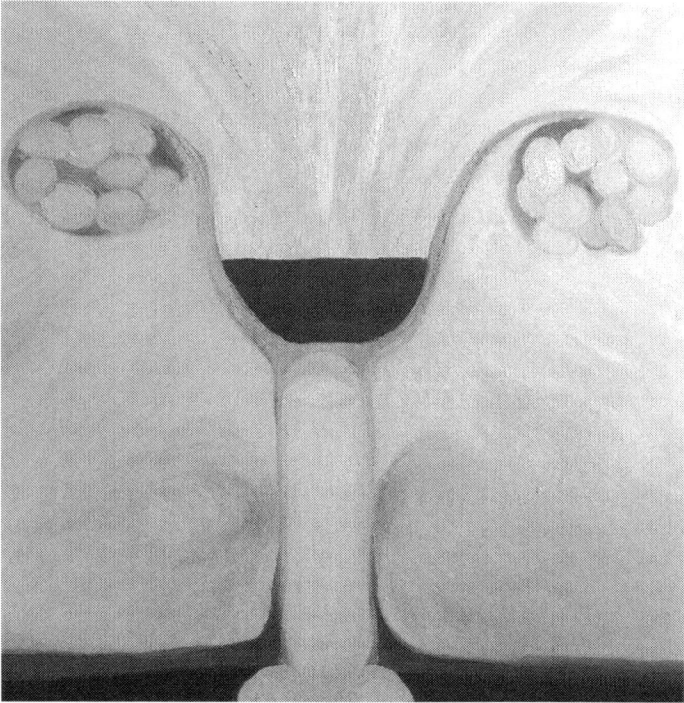

'I am a chalice of Christ; my body is a vessel for the blood of Christ'. Painting by Amanda McGregor

With all these activities developing post Christianity in Europe, and the Middle East clashing with Judaism, Christianity, Islam and Catholicism, we see the separations of faith, of love and of light. We see the will of 'man' attempting to impact on 'creation' with their own understandings of the worship of 'creation', met in man's lust and desire to intimately consume persons and bring communion and community into union in an attempt to claim back some control over creation and destiny.

In traditional relationships we see dominance and submission played out culturally, on many levels and in many faiths. More generally, when a man approaches a women, he courts her or dates her, in some faiths he may open a pathway to marriage, yet then he may step back, when she has bonded. She surrenders to her love for him as he takes control. He may take her to a place of submission simply by stepping back; this seems to passively disempower her. She feels bonded and in love, she may be in love or she may read those anxious feelings of disempowerment as 'being in love'. He may unknowingly 'feed' off her energy finding freedom and control. This dynamic in relationship is quite normal, the woman is vulnerable with her open heart, under the control of the man.

There are sometimes expressions of experience to suggest the man will take care of her with dinner and gifts, creating a surrendering of woman as they trust. However without fundamentally supporting the woman's inner truth and 'true' essence or destiny the relationship is based around his needs. The woman is vulnerable to being trapped in the boundaries of his desires and lifestyle without any ability for her to be truly supported in her 'real' sense of journey. The relationship risks becoming 'closeted' and entrapping.

A man who is dedicated to forming a meaningful relationship holds a trusted space whilst the woman's vulnerability expresses, enabling a nurturing of her authentic self and relating into the depth of the experience. He allows her sense of self to be fully heard and experienced.

In the modern day, the roles can be reversed and sometimes there is an ability to move between the roles of submission to dominance especially when a person knows they like to control their relationship and environment from a dominant perspective or when a person owns they like to experience submission. In these instances they are consciously expressed. In the expression there can be an unfolding journey back into trust and the heart and there can be a creative space of sexual expression, the heart centre allows a bonding and an experience of transformation in enabling a renewed loving connection with source. The conscious exploration of understanding is visited through strong communication, boundaries and a holding space of love, in which each other's vulnerabilities are safe to be expressed without judgement.

Looking for talents in each other and mastering leadership skills in a relationship can help to allow a holding space for growth. One person may be good at communication, another lifestyle, creativity, a particular career, wealth, spirituality, social skills or cooking. Sometimes it helps to honour the other person by giving them freedom to develop those aspects by being slightly subservient. However it is still important to know which areas you would like to focus on in growth, even if just for stress release or fun. When a dominant personality creates shadow over a weaker skill-set in a partner it can make them feel lost. It is important to acknowledge and empower an individual's movements forward on a personal level, no matter how amateur they may appear.

The merging of mission and purpose from a central place of love, creates directions beyond initial passions.

Development

There are development groups that encourage healing from abuse and from being abusive. These acts of transformation are built on the original nature of sacred communion, a safe place for transformation. The acceptance that the duality of love is met through pain allows a space for transformation in development of the energies into peace, allowing an experience of pain through the consenting of experience. The embracing of pain through consensual (con, with sensual) acts allows us to accept the more painful side of love. However to ascend the duality of pain into love we can move in a place of infinite light in the communion of the Source of Spirit or God conscious, the universal body of consciousness of God head of love. This is a place in which 'Divine Will' guides and we allow life to flow through us without attachment to pain and in a strong relationship to love. When we have an emotional sore spot we tend to channel that vibration of pain out into the world. Through the journey of resolution, the unfolding of the emotional binding energies and the release of that energy centre we can raise our vibration and shut the doors of that lower frequency, ascending into a brighter and lighter reality. Over time we can nurture and build those energies to raise us into ascension and towards a more blissful reality.

Whilst in transition into light, healing groups can be found through sex therapists, tantra, tantric massage, some magical circles and the erotic school of mysteries. These environments are designed to allow an acceptance of self, no matter the shadows, memories, feelings or desires, giving a space for persons to explore themselves, their pain and their sexuality through a safe place based on love, where the participants have a freedom of expression, role play and with a full understanding that the central point of space is held through love, non judgement, openness and acceptance. Allowing all members of the community to have a space of growth and development, a place to find their integrity, to work through their fantasies and to have release from the burdens and their

shadows, allowing a pathway in to transparency, accountability and light.

For more complicated problems of sexuality, role playing
can work effectively. In a consenting safe environment a
person can play victim or abuser or any number of roles
or archetypes to transform and heal from their stories.
Thus, when they return to the community they can project
love and positive service having exorcised some of their
darker characteristics. The ability to express without
judgement but with healthy boundaries forms a healing
and nurturing story of development that allows the light
back in and a sense of communion to be re-established
taking each person closer and closer to their relationship
with God.

The full deliverance to the God consciousness; in trusting
love and light can be understood through the journey of
healing. Jung draws a large circle with a smaller circle
inside it. The smaller circle is the individual self-absorbed
procrastinating on self-love. When on the journey of healing with the communion and others the person starts to
reconnect to the collective. As the trust comes back so
does the expansion of self, reconnecting to the wider
consciousness, the larger circle, the God consciousness.
As trust is supported the reconnection to God is established. When wanting deliverance to God and detachment
from demons or individualism, it is possible to find
commitment into the trust and surrender to God and the
collective, by re-affirming love of God, surrendering to
the consciousness of the community at large and the global community in the present day. The journey can be done

through hypnotherapy or in deep meditation, the core belief needs re-programming on a higher conscious level, **'I affirm my communion with the heart of God' 'I trust in love and light', 'I follow my heart'.** Deliverance can be carried out by various persons in 'trust' and 'understanding'. This enables the reconnection, and faith in love is re-established. People use the transformational environments of healing and expression in different ways.

The shift of living through the heart instead of through the ego can be met with resistance and fear from those attached to material wealth, status, trophy in partnership and power, as it is a surrendering into trusting relationships and growth and nurture from a deeply soulful loving position. Erotica often finds different routes of expression when living through the heart, allowing a creative pathway to enable an open and honest relationship to the universe and God conscious. Sexual surrender, through the giving over to the divine energies of creation and the bliss of euphoria experienced in the raised and elevated energies of sacred sexual experience, enables a submission to the God head of love, bathing the union in pure and divine spiritual bliss. This move to living from the heart is like a detachment from lust into the benefits of divine experience. The energies are as big as the universe and as enveloping as the divine. They bath in beauty, love and surrender to enable an expanded and God-centred connection with all that is regenerating and rejuvenating as the light of God channels through bringing inspiration and deep connection.

Living with Love

In long term relationship, the divine masculine and divine feminine are able to open themselves up to a saturating experience that is as expansive as the universe. In allowing creation to literally channel through them, they became the facilitator and the creator; a creative channel of the God-head. The experience of living with the sublime experience of relationship allows for a phenomenal experience of life, in its creation, inspiration and healthy communication, giving an open and wondrous reality that connects into oneness and the infinite portal of love; the energies so immensely powerful that hurdles are dissolved to bring in light, understanding and connection.

If one person is less developed than the other, the acceptance that not all aspects of relating can be met in a one-on-one relationship means extended safe environments can be engaged with and created for growth, development, sharing and connection. These 'understandings' have to be entered into from a place of sensitivity, trust, honour, boundary, transparency, agreement and safety, so that the beloved is fully blessed and served in honour and love, so that divinity finds a place of expression through the two persons allowing their mirroring to provide a space of union and re-union.

The interweaving of a person's energies, emotionally and spiritually, through love and light is a given space to experience in freedom. However it can bring up aspects in need of healing. Staying open to the journey, without control but in surrender to the intensity of the journey through open communication allows light, empowerment and an 'unravelling' of truth to serve and becoming enlightening. This creates a benevolence for all persons. The expression and depth of personal truth around the true nature of circumstance, sharing understandings and experience enables the communion with the collective. We are all connected in truth. We discover we can trust the surrendering to our vulnerability as the journey unravels and serves, catalysing us into a divine order of connection, union and relationship through a recognition of a heart connection, emotional, spiritual, physical or intellectual connection. Recognising connections and communicating the nature of relationships allows a conscious accountability. Identifying the true nature of a relationship informs the pathway and outcome, unravelling the complications into clarity and understanding. Forming a pathway in which the shadows of manipulation, control and deception fade away in to the past. By being accountable, honourable, open, transparent, with healthy boundaries allows many complications and hurdles to be overcome. Understanding another's pain on a deep and integral level often is a mirror of one's own complications. Sitting deep inside one's self, confronting the true nature of circumstance, the pain and reality of being, enables self empathy. Self empathy brings self acceptance and process which leads to change, healing and transformation. Confronting another's deep pain and allowing yourself to be present with their core wounds enables a deep love to serve with medicinal properties. This level of love requires deep care and attention but serves to create deep bonds and profound relationships. How do I really feel about being me, how do I see myself in another?

Ask yourself, 'Is my relationship fully open to my true feelings, my mission, purpose, love, heart or journey?' Affirm - **'I trust in the love and the light of open, non-judgemental expression. Communion in love will enable a free expression of all my needs and desires'**

Rebalancing the Energies into Masculine and Feminine Harmony

The desire to arrive back at a present place of loving openness and oneness in co-creation, leads us to trust and surrender in the communicative journey of change and transformation. To bring union back into our lives, we allow our feelings to be expressed and the impact of others on our psychology and physical lives to be fully understood. By not judging or blaming and by staying open, we are able to allow transformation in, creating a space to raise awareness and consciousness, through our feelings being respected, understood and expressed, with active adjustments to help uplift and bring in change. Slowly in time we may need to make adjustments, changing the way we create boundaries, respect boundaries, look at the types of energies that inform our relationships. Being conscious of the components of communicative energies that form our relationships, we can help to manage directives, emotive and desires. Being open about how physical, emotional, spiritual and intellectual aspects interrelate and connect, allows the pathways of development.

At the early stages of a relationship, we can assess how we feel about another by recognising our feelings whilst we are in another's presence in silence. We are able to manage all the energies that motivate and connect with the fundamental aspect of the relationship. Those feelings inform us of how safe we are, how much joy we feel, how comfortable we are. We can then go deeper on a journey of sharing and expression looking at wants, needs and desires. However on the journey of relationship we may want to change the energetic dynamics and start managing the open channels of experience or the possible pathways of potential relationship. For instance a person may want to embrace more adventure, holidays, children, sharing a home or close 'desire' or 'lust' with another because of being in a committed marriage or partnership. We can change the dynamics by moving through archetypes and realising that the universe is working through us, we trust in the relationships that evolve, bring journey, light living, we can invest in the persons that magnify those energetic exchanges. We have different roles in the way we relate, there is mother, lover, wife, mistress, fool, friend or father, lover, player, male mistress. We can discuss ways of changing the management of these characteristics and we can find ways to bring harmony and peace to corrupted relationships. The archetypes can create areas of lack in themselves that can have an effect on relating. So a person who is fully embracing mother energies may not be present in lover role with her partner, or someone fully in mistress may not be able to step into mother, these energies need to be integrated, held in a holding position of the Holy Trinity of Mother, Father and inner Child in which they can find their centre and depth of experience in love (the inner child holds space for the erotica of lover).

The trinity is also effective in same sex relationships. Due to our androgyny and anima, in which we have both male and female roles as individuals, we hold space in both male and female genders with the inner child our catalyst for development and trust. The union of these parts in peace and commitment brings pathways of partnership that reflect out, in who we attract and relate to.

We often are attracted to another, from an act of deep compassion in self love, mirroring an emotion we have and experience in the other person. This can happen on a soul level; maybe loneliness, emptiness, adventure, intellectual understanding. We need to heal our sense of lack or pain to form consistently loving relationships in which we don't need to extend ourselves to experience something beyond our own expansion.

The way two persons arrive at a state of relationship is very different. A man tends to bond in the journey of relating over time, when he can see the path is free to develop a physically expansive, safe and happy relationship. Women bond when they sense the signals that they are connected, happy and will open their hearts through physical contact and emotional involvement. Women will often open their hearts or fall in love when they emotionally bond or have sex, whereas men need to see the long term development for their hearts to open. This is why one night stands are so complex.

The woman often sees sexual activity as a foundation to creating an unconditionally loving relationship. She sees sex as the process of bonding and when mixed with emotional connection, she sees it as primary in relating with the components of longevity. To a certain level, with an open heart, she is able to love unconditionally., she fully allows the man in to her personal space, to be held in love in the long term, she naturally forms deep attachment to nurture this connection.

A man often sees sex as pleasure. He can easily detach and can be casual in extending his understanding to seeing things from a female perspective. He may project, 'we just had fun, it was just a meeting' and will easily let go or depart from the experience. A women will think about the man for twenty four hours a day, maybe beyond two weeks, the man often struggles to understand the depth of experience a women has; when her heart opens through love making; the experience completely overwhelms her whole psychology for weeks. A conscious man will allow the woman's psychology to remain true, he will also be true to himself. He will allow her to love him in her way but he will be clear about the pathway forward and allow communication to openly find development, clarity and healthy boundaries.

A man takes responsibility in his heart when he sees a future and that he is being loved unconditionally over time. When he realises how important the woman is to him, how much she gives to him and how nurtured, inspired, sexually attracted, emotionally connected, elevated or uplifted he feels in respect to her. He takes on a role of holding the relationship, giving an architecture to the couple's pathway, he often opens his heart when he is at a point of fully respecting a woman's nature and ability to integrate love, care and erotica.

A women has to learn to feel vulnerable and trust in her 'attached' connection with the man and her experience of open hearted love, without doubting her feelings. She must detach from expectation, remain constant, open, in her truth and in her flow. A man needs to trust in the experience of her.

In the early stages of two people meeting, fear can play out due to past let-downs. This normally communicates around worry of manipulation, rejection and control. These elements can be overwhelming. One person who lives in fear or doubt will create that in the other, as they will project onto the person they are relating to, this may dominate and form emotional reactivity. So if two people present lightly to each other, that will be their experience, we mirror the other. If either party brings the relationship 'down', to a place of fear or worry about control, manipulation, a past relationship, the whole affair tends to fall to a lower sense of experience and operate on that level. To keep the relationship on a high, it is important to nurture spaces of activity with fun and light humour so that the getting to know each other period is balanced with not too much heavy emotional unearthing but a reasonable amount of connectivity, emotionally, physically, intellectually and spiritually. Recognising the connecting areas of conversation and experience helps to enhance the journey and elevate and uplift beyond fear or heart defence. A serious relationship generally needs the safety of monogamy for both parties to share their vulnerabilities in intimacy, emotionally and in naked truth about their true nature. This safety is very important. The safety houses growth, play, creativity and experience. In the long term there are no real safety nets to relationships: there is only an honest and open journey in which the two parties can express their feelings, boundaries and be direct in an honest and communicative way that leads them to experience their union in happiness. The choice of nurturing happiness, allows an honourable growth in that it enables peace and expansion. Two people may decide to depart or change the boundaries of their relationship; if done in honour they will express this openly and honestly without disempowering or violating the boundaries of the other. Disempowerment through judging, blocking or juggling others can create great anxiety and depression in another if it is not agreed. Think very carefully before instigating this type of 'control'. To honour each other in separating it is possible to take on the responsibility of giving emotional space, peace and freedom; this can be liberating for both parties. When one or another party feels threatened in a break-up, they may block, close down or push away. This can be very destructive on all areas of lifestyle. To be non-threatening it is possible to make safe, conscious and liberating decisions to enable benevolence, security, communication and detachment for all persons.

In traditional western marriage if the man is sexually active beyond the boundaries of one partner he will often remain in the primary relationship unless the partner asks for this. He sees this as unconditional love and often expects unconditional love in return. However, a women often sees the bonding sexually as a sacred space and often cannot extend her unconditional love to the thought of him with another partner or other women; this is because she relates to intimacy in love and bonding. This can be addressed in some cultures and relationships if the women involved are fully honoured with time, quality of experience, integrity and a sense of value and respect. They then find a pathway in to loving third parties. When there is estrangement, the man or woman risks breaking the emotional bond with their partner by straying, or lying; the break of trust tends to centre on a mistrust in dependability and understanding. The distrust in dependability is the main cause for concern. A person in intimate relationship needs to feel safe and protected and will often choose their partner based on a sense of safety. If a person breaks that feeling or experience through having a secret affair, they break a fundamental value in relating.

Betrayal is when a person meets their own needs or desires with a sacrifice to another's feelings or security. They know they are acting against your feelings or wishes, they thereby act to step over you. They may do this through manipulation, deception or control. Betrayal leaves a trail, it creates inherited behaviour as it challenges and destroys self esteem. Those characteristics are then passed on through projection. The belittling is an undermining of value, a squashing of emotional impact, silencing and sometimes closeting. A person that betrays them self or another magnifies the impact of their position. This can be likened to throwing a stone in to a lake: the circles or impact of the fall of the stone magnifies through the entire emotional water body, the circles of effect get larger over time. The issues can cause a psychological death as the relationship looses a sense of real 'connection' with persons involved. Those affected can loose the integrity in the journey of connection, they are placed in the illusion of separation to oneness. The true nature of relationship becomes buried, 'sex turns in to the sea'; it looses meaning becoming watered down. When relating to someone with a deep soul connection sometimes it is possible to heal, communicate and transform the relationship beyond the problems, this requires a dedicated unearthing of personal truths and transparency.

To manage an understanding around male and female differences, it is important to fully understand the different nature of needs of both the man and the woman. How does each person relates to freedom; is that a psychological feeling based need or a physical need? Is each person able to be monogamous to one person on a level of physical penetrative sex? If freedom of sexual fantasy or erotica is given does that need to be played out physically in life or can it simply be a freedom of thought? Where do the boundaries lie? How does each person bring trust and security to the relationship? How do they support transparency and empowerment? Are they able to recognise the difference between different forms of intimacy and sex? Are they able to hold space in love for growth and change?

Most people crave sensual loving intimacy but they are happy with just one partner for sexual relationship. So most couples can create agreements of monogamous sex with more liberal encounters of emotional intimacy and sensual care. Adhering to boundaries and working out the details creates trust and understanding.

Often one person seeks more clarity in the relationship than the other; they will have a clearer idea of the problems that seem to emerge. They act as the reflector, helping to bring an inward understanding to growth and development.

Generally, a person's journey of development will often reveal a sense of 'private garden'; areas of their psychology in which they have found freedom to develop emotional relationships, experiences with erotica, pornography, online experiences and meeting inspiring people. These can become 'distractions' from being present and if not careful, can feed the ego. A person's private garden can hold areas of deception, in which by sharing concerns directly with a partner, works through to a transformational place of understanding. This element can take decades to find peace with but with a space for transparency, non-judgement, boundaries and understanding, these elements can be explored and understood in primary partnership.

Trusting in the collective consciousness can allow transformation in; the journey back to oneness and union instructs from a deeper truth. Allowing the true nature of the union to be fully understood by persons and for those elements to enter into a transformational position of change by confronting and talking about deeper issues, can help to bring love and focussed commitment back into the primary relationship. Thus, by allowing love to be a dominating factor and by fully confronting the grounds in which the relationship was built and the pathology of change away from certain archetypes can help to address and deal with disruptive elements. The main area to look at is in emotional complexity: to be able to express deep feelings and be able to be fully heard through those thoughts and understandings.

Being emotionally dependable through loving, listening and actively addressing another's emotional chaos, unconditionally and without judgement becomes the most important part of a long term relationship.

Relationships that work over lifelong periods of time, have their own way of emotional transformation, the couple has a way of opening up their emotions and allowing understanding in by being gentle, loving, humorous and responsive. The element of emotional transformation is key in a happy relationship, look at how you find resolution in partnership, how do you uplift each other beyond your hurdles. Being able to reach each other emotionally, tolerate a deep emotional unearthing, hear each other so as to allow transformation in, helps to uplift, find new directions and ascend emotionally to a lighter state of being, no matter how complex the circumstance. This developed sense of awareness allows a long term pathway into happiness and peaceful living.

A Meditation to bring in Harmony in to the Self and a Relationship

To raise the energies to a relationship suited to honour it is important to look at the components of the energies of marriage. There is a shift into 'familiarity' this is intimate but often less desire-based or lustful. Shifting in to a more familiar form of relating can create many problems in harmony, so we can rebalance the energies in a relationship to adjust into an expressive area of relationship development.

The God the Father represents the masculine parts, whereas the Holy Spirit, Shakina represents the female energies, the Goddess, the Mother Earth. We bond Father, Sky, Air, with Mother Earth, and we allow the Holy Trinity of the God, Father, Son, Jesus, and Holy Spirit/Shakina to combine with a peaceful water energy to bond. The female part needs to be constructively larger than masculine, 62 percent greater. The female energies can be embodied through water, so it is possible to visualise a waterfall cascading from Father Sky, down to a deep tranquil warm pool on the ground at Mother Earth. Visualising an abundance of growth, beauty and the warm sun of your heart projecting into the vision, allows you to embody the sensations and energies. Allow yourself to arrive at the pool and bathe in the sacred waters, baptising yourself in the energies of God the Father with Shakina, Mother Earth Goddess, by allowing the energies to consume you. By bathing in the waters you allow the rebalance of nurture in grace through a rebalancing of archetypal identities. If your relationship is in a position of change and transition you can use this space to invite your partner into the sacred pool, to discuss emotional aspects freely and directly, giving time to properly 'hear' soulful responses. It is very important to not project an idea of what you think the other person may say. Wait for responses and relate on a deep soul level of deeper truth, allowing a conversation to develop about concerns and elements that need looking at. Allow the true nature of experience to play out and the outcome to be properly heard and attended to through acceptance and discussion.

4 THE SACRED RIVER OF TRUTH

The Sacred River of Truth

I often use a visualisation of God's Garden, in which I bathe in the sacred waters. Below is a guided meditation process used to release emotions that may create attachment, to enable a process in to trust or collaboration.

"The Sacred River of Truth" Meditation

Please sit comfortably, lying or leaning back. Take your attention to your breathing, visualising breathing white light oxygen into your lungs and down into your blood stream. Keep drawing the energy in, through your body, into your legs and arms. When you feel you have filled your body and soul with white light, invoking a soul connection of truth, begin to go on the journey to the Sacred River of Truth.

If for a moment we imagine walking down a path in a woody glade, the light shines through the trees and as we get to the edge of the natural land, the grass becomes thicker and the trees fade away to open into untouched natural land; the grass is deep green, soft to the foot, so soft you can be barefoot. There is a beautiful, clear, warm water river running out of some rocks through a glade of peaceful fertile land that connects to the sacred energy of Source and the heart of God.

Today is a warm day. You are able to relax and unwind; slowly you relax into being by the warm water, dipping your toes in. In time, you feel the healing properties of the water; slowly unwinding, you lower yourself in to the water, feeling how the warm water holds you, lifts away your emotions, enables you to find peace. Slowly allow yourself to drift, visualise bathing yourself through that deep warm, light source energy, swimming through the gentle current allowing the water to sweep away any negativity. Spend time simply allowing the water to hold you, closing your eyes, immersing yourself into the peaceful waters. Then ask the river to baptise your life experience in Spiritual Truth, asking that all your emotional states be grounded in the true nature of your spiritual experience that you set out on this life journey.

Ask the Sacred River of Truth what is the most important aspect of your learning in this lifetime, listening for the response. Allow yourself to enjoy the freedom of being in the river, freely floating. It's a warm day, it's a very private place where you can freely be yourself.

Now I am going to invite you to cleanse through your heart emotions, thinking in relation to your life experiences in the present time. We will take one emotion at a time: we will visualise an object, stone or a symbol to represent that emotion and we will slowly breath through the emotion and the layers of the emotion, allowing the emotion to dissolve and the true nature of the experience to reveal itself.

Imagine being in your heart and ask your heart to give you a vision of an object relating to your experience of the following word —

Justice

Imagine an object, symbol or stone that represents 'justice', then take that object or symbol to the Sacred River of Truth and bathe the visual imagery in it allowing the image to dissolve with every deep breath, until the feelings are swept away. Then ask the Sacred River of Truth for the true nature of the experience of 'justice' and listen to its response, breathing into the moments as you wait for a reply. The response should ground you in understanding the true nature of how you have experienced your feelings from a place of spiritual truth rather than human truth. This should release you from your negative feelings, taking you to a place of Source and freedom. Keep bathing the visual object until it dissolves and you feel strong in your understanding of the emotional complexity of the word.

Then do the same with the following words:

Emotion	Vision	Spiritual Truth
Justice		
Humility		
Appreciation		
Compassion		
Understanding		
Forgiveness		

The Emotional Centre of the Sacral

Freeing the Sacral Centre is key to our self-acceptance and experiencing the full dynamics of our identity. However, it is also the centre of our emotional world and our emotional intelligence. It is important not to underestimate the capacity of use of emotional intelligence. The sacral is a very powerful connecting point to Source and with that connection we also gain the gift of deep understanding, compassion and wisdom: universal understanding. When this area is developed we can become kinaesthetic and therefore 'feel' our way into truth of spiritual experience and help our perception to become aligned to 'true' 'nature' of 'experience'. This area is like a labyrinth of understanding, as if creating order in our library of personal experience and information or emotions. The more developed we become the more sophisticated our feeling are but let's look at our negative emotions because when we become very spiritual they are the hardest to accept within our body.

Emotion	Vision	Spiritual Truth
Anger		
Disappointment		
Violation		
Undermining		
Jealousy		
Deception		
Hurt		

Setting the Sacred River as a Default

From a philosophical perspective connecting to Source is the path to enlightenment. This action connects us to the universe in all its dimensions and complexities and helps us inter-react from a place of light and love. Here we are able to ground ourselves in wisdom and understanding in a way that surpasses anxiety, depression and negativity.

Once we have worked out the true nature of our experiences from a point of the Sacred River of Truth and how we relate to the world through them, we can then invite the Sacred River of Truth to run freely through our energy systems. By inviting the default of Source energy to catalyse us into a grounded state of awareness we allow ourselves to operate from a place of light and love continuously. This especially helps us deal in the long term with rage and anger.

To do this, visualise floating on the current of the river, lying on your back as the river runs through you. Open your Crown chakra at the top of your head and allow the energy to integrate with your body, pouring into the top of your head and allowing it to find its way around your brain, the skin in between your skull and hair, your eyes and your neck. Then breathe it down into your body through your lungs into your blood stream and down through your digestive system into your pelvis. On the out breath be aware of letting go of any tensions, fears or worries, letting this energy float away into the sky to be taken care of by the angels.

Then from your pelvis allow the energy to build up with every breath until you have a ball of energy like a sphere the size of a ball sitting in your pelvis. When this energy feels strong and pro-active, allow it like a white energetic sacral snake to crawl up the back of your spine into your head and back out of your Crown chakra. Then start breathing through your body allowing the white energy of the sacred river to move through your whole torso and out the other side through your Root chakra, connecting with the source point of the river.

Anchoring

Allow yourself to anchor this experience by holding your little finger and connecting to a chosen area of your brain, with a symbolic vision of an object or symbol, so that when you need to be reminded of your grounded essence you are able to activate yourself to ground your emotions.

The Shadow Self

This is relating from a point of insecurity, fear, pain, resentment or anxiety. Sometimes after a challenge we can suddenly feel like we are falling inside, as if the ground has fallen away. We are aware that anything we say, do and attempt may end in further failure. We have to look at the catalyst to attempt to deconstruct a way to unhook the ensuing damage and find our feet so that we can move forward in the world; surrendering to the fall can give stronger grounding in the end. Speaking from this place means we are likely to construct sentences based on insecurity which appears to an audience as if we are unable to be secure and present. So how did we get to this point and what do we need to do?

Anxiety is a symptom of dysfunction in the mind. Anxiety is caused by not having enough information to process your situation or reality; by realising you don't have enough facts or the whole truth to be able to understand or process the situation, if you are not able to gain them presently, tell your mind not to try to process when it can't construct an understanding of the situation. Ask it to let go of the situation, person, or reality and be at peace.

Falling is a sensation inside caused by the sensation of the perceived inner security or ground going from under our feet; it is a feeling of insecurity. One has to wonder if we were on solid ground in the first instance for the situation or area of challenge/conflict to have arisen, but in moving forward in life one has to take on the risk of exploration in trusting the process of inter-relating to create possible pathways into future opportunities and the creation of security. When looking at our foundations and sense of security we have to look at whether or not we had developed secure foundations in ourselves or not. We have to look at the nature of the relationships in both work and personally that we are attracting. We then have to look at the security of the others we are relating to. Our inner insecurity can be magnified by emotional black holes of being severely let down in the past. If we are triggered to re-experience an aspect of disempowerment which leads to a sense of insecurity, the sense of falling can be magnified due to past hurts being unconsciously triggered. An emotional black hole is when there seems no end to our distress and sense of falling, as we have perhaps fallen into a 'Void'. The void is infinite space of emotional darkness, the opposite of source. For us to climb out of this experience I find it best to reconsider 'values' and also re-look at anxiety and trust in choices and processes.

The value aspect is important in aligning to intentions and ways of dealing and living with relationship. Your values tend to dictate your expectations of behavior and how you stay buoyant. Every person has their own way of relating in this way. They also guide in the right area of career success. That which is important to us tends to become the important aspect in Emotional Black Holes. These are the points in you that in life we call our 'buttons'. They come into action when we are challenged in a way we feel is detrimental to our being; we tend to 'act out' emotionally and go into anger and resentment, chan-nelling as much of that energy at the person who has (through our perception) misunderstood, mistreated, or misrepresented us, or simply let us down. There is often a fundamental pitfall of insecurity underneath the situation, in which anger may be used as a defense by the affected party because of the perceived threat. There may be a sense of overwhelm, in which it seems impossible to communicate the vastness of the concepts or feelings experienced. This feeling of being let down can come as a shock encouraging a demonstrating of strength in presence and assertiveness. However that level of anger can be disempowering as it shows an area of emotional immaturity in which you are psychologically not in control. Emotions have to be processed but they don't have to be channelled through out-of-control expression, however our nature is to channel the energy of them through conversation or shouting! After that we process them psychologically, then release them by letting go. Emotions are energy with different vibrational frequencies. The lower frequencies of anger and resentment etc.. can only be made into light and love by processing through psychological understanding, different healing processes, Brandon Bays the Journey, E.F.T., Sacred River of Truth, massaging or tapping meridian points or changing energetic vibration with healing or high vibration energy, Reiki or similar therapies. No amount of emotional expression without dealing with or confronting the 'true' nature can release them, so it becomes important to 'see' or 'feel' what is 'true'. However we can choose not to take things personally or be defensive, we can decide to not give energy to offense or allow judgements to escalate, we can choose to let another's opinions remain with them.

To fully be present emotionally in 'truth' is a journey of 'integrity' which can give us the benefit of holistically keeping us spiritually, psychologically and emotionally in order and connected to the light and love of Source. However when we are in full flow giving it 'all' as our buttons are being pressed, what is 'true' as an intervention when freely expressing or channelling emotions? It's all fine to understand it logically but when someone presses your buttons what is the intervention and does one get to a stage of having no buttons, ever? We can be infinite in lightness, however we can also walk the other way and be infinite and limitless in darkness. It's normal for people to have a few 'reactive emotional buttons'. These channel an infinite amount of energy in darkness, however they are normally attached to maps of emotional concepts, that when unravelled, free the person from the sore spot. When I work one-to-one with people clairvoyantly they literally look like an opening into a vortex of black hole in their emotional body. When I am in session with a client I put in the grounding, light or inner security to address the issues, so that they have a platform to trans-form their emotional energy into infinite light. I do this by assessing the values they have in their belief systems and in their higher consciousness and then channel Source energy into the space connecting them to their inner Source energy and infinite light being, transforming the situation. The question is, 'How does one deal with this on one's own?' Well, to deal with the issues, one has to give oneself permission to fully be heard and seen 'in one's power' which means being seen, letting go of limit-ing beliefs. Therefore changing belief systems to 'I am able to be seen in power', although perceived by people to be misunderstood and not seen for the true person, others can 'act out' due to self-imposed limit and weakness, which means others see an advantage point for exploitation. They can step out of their belief in you, as you don't believe in yourself, by projecting limited beliefs out. To act out is to leave integrity temporarily and step into another role, as if acting. This of course is due to insecurity appearance, so there is a sense of being out of control in the issue.

This element of undermine and reactivity or acting out, can play out in many different ways. Especially in development phases of recovery, as limited beliefs become more obvious. The experience can seem like a circle, taking us all into a sense of feeling low. Choosing to step out of the drama allows the projections, judgements, opinions to find light.

For Example - To repair the damage is to bring this emotional issue to its source point, by bathing the feelings of a sense of 'under-mind' in the Sacred River of Truth, of which the voice came back, 'you are in your truth'- a message from the sacred emotional centre. The light and love are able to flood in and the affirmation 'I am able to be seen in my power' takes hold. Other affirmations can be presented for all sorts of issues: it is important to go to the Sacred River of Truth with an empty head, free from thoughts.

To take on affirmations to the higher consciousness, repeat affirmation continuously, whilst crossing wrists and ankles and interlocking fingers. The stronger cross-over position, of left over right or right over left when arms and legs are held in strength, is the most important posture. This can change every time you come to do the exercise. This exercise cuts through your brain and goes into your higher consciousness, the big brother of your psychology and emotional centre, and aligns to spirituality. Hypnotherapy is also a good way of changing limited beliefs. Kinesiology is good for sourcing problems and finding direction in avenues in healing. Kinesiology can also bring clarity that change has happened. Another way is to look in to a mirror, looking deep in to your soul whilst repeating the affirmations.

Is it possible to get past the black holes of emotional reactivity? I think reactivity is often formed around patterns of behavior, so I think one has to accept that management comes from non-violent communication, humour and finding a lighter way of expression over time. The trouble-shooting of all black holes is a long journey, so using the higher power of Source energy and stability can bring emotional peace and psychological well-being.

Bullying

Any sort of undermining is considered bullying. Bullying is effective because of a person's insecurity, and the bully's stubbornness in getting their own way. There is often a vulnerability that the bully sees in their victim on which they focus. They are then able to feed an untruth or magnify a sense of personal concern, which the person with low self-esteem buys into, by feeling less than they are. Becoming aware of which untruth the bully is focusing on helps to gain back control; positive affirmations can be used to self- validate away from concerns and this enables a stronger position. A stalker or abuser that is infinite in their attempts to dis-empower has an emotional black hole of insecurity. They claim power over their victim by projecting on them their own insecurity. This makes the bully empowered and energised. A person who will only do everything on their terms and within their own comfort zone can be bullying; they often live through their ego as they don't trust the world beyond them. Affirming, 'I deserve to be seen in my power and in my light', is a way of helping us deal with the persons that prey on our vulnerabilities. Dealing with projections early on can keep control over a situation. We can do this through communication by asserting our feelings, vulnerabilities and impact of the others' actions and activities on ourselves. Expressing the whole context of the experience, the feelings and the impact or effect, whilst keeping an anchor in personal values and senses of empowerment and expectation through relating can help to create a pathway of growth through the experience. This kind of expression should be without blame, 'I feel...'

- Express your boundaries

- How it feels for the person to have ignored those boundaries

- The impact of their actions on you, through feelings and physical implications

- What is needed to rectify the situation

- Express preferred values in conduct when relating, adhering to benevolent activity

This means openly expressing personal codes of honour, values, boundaries and adjustments needed to make the situation more peaceful.

There are other conscious or spiritually intelligent energies that a person can carry in their soul purpose, or soul plan. Although we can accommodate hundreds of soul frequency energies in our processes, below we have the basic ones. We can see the colour through clairvoyance, more in the next chapter, Soul Mapping.

Communication skills - yellow

Development and growth - green

Intellectual analysis; e.g. law or finance - light blue (not in the diagram)

Creative - Orange or red/yellow

Compassion or passion - red

Protection - Red/brown

When the energies are in flow, they can be felt and intuitively seen creating an energetic figure of eight in the horizontal direction at all the major energy centres, with a clear flow that allows expansion and development. This then is able to grow into high-level performance, when all energy centres are free-flowing and at Source point. If a person is too absorbed by security and insecurity they will show a red colour in their aura.

It is possible to see how the collaborative energies are working by anchoring one or another hand with the name of the persons involved, as if holding mini imaginary people. With loose hands, feel the nature of their relation-ship by feeling the energy patterns of how they relate, by looking to 'see', and then feel the way the relationship is operating. When both hands come together, physical inti-macy is normally present, when they bounce off each other the energies may be like a magnet repelling. Through this technique it is possible to tell how often the two persons see each other and the nature of their rela-tionship, what holds the relationship back and the likely pathway forward.

The flow of activity in a person's aura is anti-clockwise; the areas are specific and normally logical. I find the person's unfolding story to be spoken through their soul in deep truth and accuracy, which allows me to gain an insight that their own mind or psychology would misin-terpret or overlook. I always invite feedback and response to my perception and findings; it is part of the process of clarity and clearing. This method is a short-cut way of really helping a person to process their life quickly and effectively, leaving them in their flow and lightness with strong platforms of inner security and dependability.

How do we nourish and nurture Bliss and plug in to diamond light energy resources?

The nourishment and nurture of this energy field can be tended to through meditation, Emotional Freedom Technique, 'The Sacred River of Truth' as mentioned in this book, reconnecting with 'source' through breath work and opening oneself to becoming a channel of light and by deeply integrating with the God consciousness of 'Creation' or the universal body of consciousness. Other nurturing qualities can be satisfied through counselling, a healthy diet, sunshine, natural light, sex, earthing (spending time with bare feet on the earth), nature, active listening, stillness, permission to do nothing and soul mapping.

The next chapter describes ways of looking deeper in to your soul or another's. This way of seeing was taught to me by the conscious universe over many years, every person I saw had exactly the same structure to their energy field. After giving 4,500 sessions I became very clear on the different energy frequencies that I was working with. I have put the next chapter together to help you in to the energy structure. The chakras are the coloured circles running centrally down the body, they are the main energy centers to work from. Please use a mirror to see into the self and to take on all affirmation in to the higher conscious.

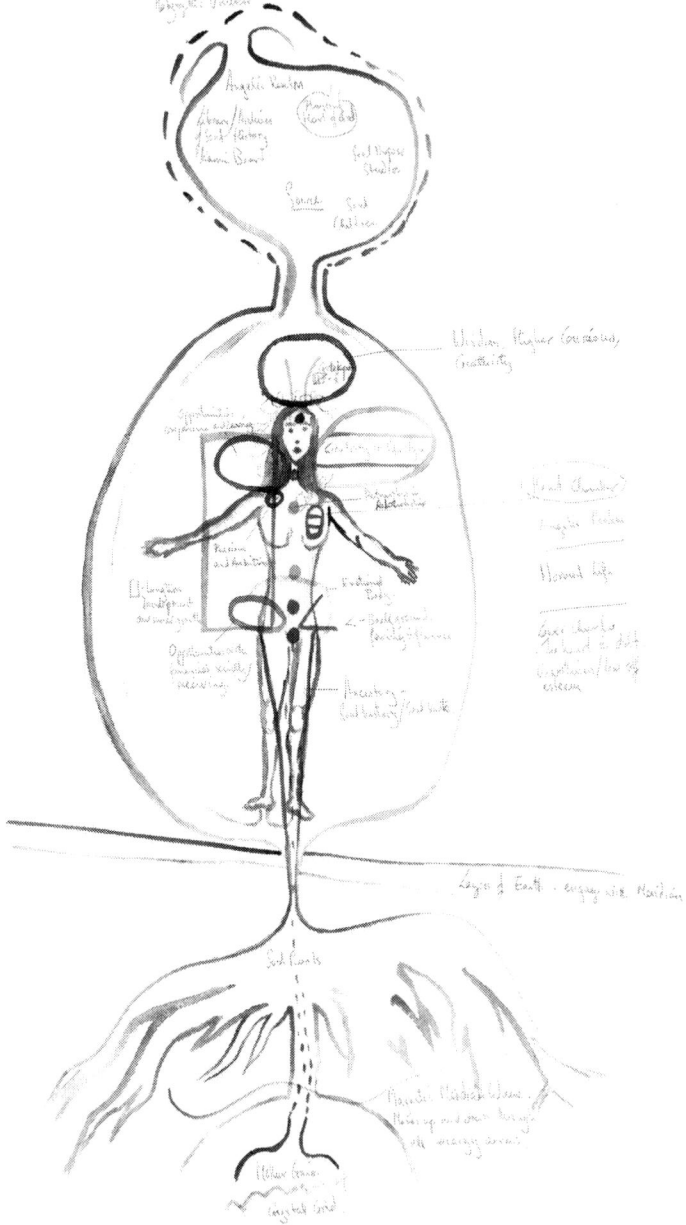

5 SOUL MAPPING

Reading the Soul Energies

To begin, we scan the energy system of the whole body with our hands, ten inches away from the physical body, feeling, sensing and looking at how strong and secure the chakra energies are and the areas I have focussed on in the diagram. I check in with family and work anti-clockwise around the body. This is because long term vision is above the heart side shoulder, so all areas have to flow into this point eventually. To look at the self, it is possible to sit in front of a mirror whilst tuning in to one's own energetic field.

Family

When reading the soul I start with the green < arrow
shaped symbol. This is the area of family and here we can
see the position of father and mother, simply by feeling
how they are placed within or without boundaries. I find
there is a spiritual link into a lighter, more abstract energy
if one has passed. The important factors around the area
of family are boundaries, because if the emotional body
does not hold clear boundaries the person carries that
issue for life. So it is important to talk through any undermining element or dynamic that compromises the person
you are reading for, to see what can be done to create
healthy boundaries.

The boundary line runs energetically as if the person was
pregnant and you can feel a literal line in their energy
system. Those persons who overstep the 'mark', cross the
line and all show up as invasive to the person's boundaries and personal emotional space. The person has a
right to be clear on how they feel without question from
another. Their feelings should be heard and their
emotional space respected. When there are a lot of family
issues coming up, there is an energetic focus in this area;
all energy seems to be drawn into a kind of energetic
vacuum around family. The area around and in front of
the stomach holds areas of void, or emotional black hole.
These energy centres need healing and closure. The reading releases the problems through acknowledging the
emotional layers and the compromises faced. By hearing
a full understanding of the dynamics, heartache and prob-

lems encountered due to the individuals and family dynamics, we are able to release the person from the problem. If they are in a present situation in the family they have created, their own children and maybe falling out with their partner, we can adjust through the heart space; the heart chamber. I really only use this space for reference for biological family.

Root Chakra

The Root Chakra runs down from the pelvis into the ground, seen here as a navy blue V. The doorway into reading it is through the red circle, the Root Chakra. Here we can see how secure the person is. If we feel into the Root Chakra and vertically down, we can feel how strong the foundation energies are. The person may be having a moment of temporary doubt or they may be facing radical doubt; if in radical doubt, the energy drops right down into the blue V. The stories we tune in to here are from a soul level and often involve past life regression. If someone is in radical doubt it means there are aspects of their relationships, their belief systems and the way their environment is constructed that are not authentically based on solid ground, they will experience insecurity. Their journey forward is in connecting with truth, true nature, economic integrity, authentic relationships and home. There can be many complications and hurdles in this path way as many aspects of the world are not built on straightforward systems of truth. Aspects such as the economy, politics and marketing techniques, which means all these aspects need to be processed and digested and related to from a place of authentic understanding for the person to move forward. To put in strong foundations, we have to mould the environment to create strong platforms of growth: this can be done through support, energy and making strong choices.

So we start with relationship and the person's own values and why they have chosen to relate in certain ways. We clear any undermining judgement from others, by giving back the energy they have dumped onto the person, or send it out to the universe. This 'dumping' on tends to create the insecurity. We are then in a position to rebuild a world around the values from which the person chooses to operate. This then goes on to extend into communications; communications or the 'word' is the first avenue of creation when connecting with others and here we see communications leading to security.

e.g. love, compassion, kindness, understanding, dependability, openness, freedom, honour, inspiration, humour, lightness etc.

Communications

This is the yellow oval to the left of centre above the pelvis. The connecting with others on a similar path, agreeing on similar values, starts to allow a journey to unfold, in development, security and love. The sharing of the pains, compassion, the challenges, the hurdles, or simply the understanding of skill sets, talents and character, enables doorways, pathways and opportunities to open up in the alignment of interests, the beginning of an understanding of passions, missions, desires and wants for a shared vision to work towards. So communications naturally lead into relationship and work opportunities and a sense of development in working 'project', in initiating and catalysing dreams and visions to enter into a 'development phase'. In this section we can see which persons are effective collaborators, friends and colleagues. The energies will express themselves: I tune into the area with my fingers and ask for the information to come to me and I then listen to that information and then express it to the person I am working with.

The sacral centre, seen here as a red-orange energy, is the seat of creativity. Here we can see how confident a person is in expressing themselves and how creative they are in that self-expression. They need to feel inner security in their sacral to be open and 'themselves'. The finding of their voice means sometimes an energetic link needs to be re-aligned to their throat chakra (through the channelling of (Reiki/light) energy). A secure and confident person can be visualised in their sacral, they are seen as able to speak out and create expansive pathways through the oval energy, so as to expand their area of talk, education or sharing to a global position. As time goes on, there should be a feeling of unfolding, a sense of a coil moving right through the development energy.

Development

The development energy can be seen as a rectangular green box. The green energy depicts growth. This is where the energy builds and needs a level of strength in working process; the energy has to be constructive and continue to be fed into. Any sense of vacuum can interfere and destroy its growth. Invasion, corruption and interference of other people have to be cleared, by asking them to step away, by not sharing, by repositioning their placement. In the place of development it is important to have connected, authentic relationships which allow growth, nourishment and nurture, in which all skill sets are expanded upon and in which support is given to enable solid foundations of activity. By taking care of any weak areas, confronting fears and weaknesses, enables a transformation into a stronger path of growth.

Opportunities and Passions

At the top of 'green rectangle of development' you will see an oval green symbol; this is the area of opportunities. Opportunities are a complex set of circumstances, felt by the acknowledgement of the small red circle of 'passion' seen on the right shoulder. Opportunities are about the desire for 'new'; new relationship, new job, new life. Opportunities are always available in the world but need to come from an organic alignment with mission, self-love, dream and vision, otherwise they fall into 'lust' and remain an opportunity rather than a reality. So the way I deal with opportunities is to check in with passions, alignment with the heart energy, long term vision and mission. Passion energy can feel stuck, undermined, sticky, corrupted, unheard, closeted or can be too much around opportunities. So to begin we loosen this energy.

Freeing Passions

To free passions, or any stuck energy, tune in to the emotions in this area by using the fingers as antennae; acknowledge the emotions, share them, and then see what's underneath them. Keep going, breathing through the layers of emotions, until you get to a feeling of 'free' energy or the energetic horizontal, figure of eight.

For instance, tuning in to someone -

I feel you have tried everything to share your self-expression but it keeps getting put away and closeted. It feels like you are being hidden. Question to their soul- 'who is hiding you?' Follow the energetic link - Oh, let's go to family. Yes, there is an issue with your mother and father; something happened to you, they couldn't face it, so they put it to one side, they put you to one side. They have never re-embraced you. The dynamics shifted from that day on. You need to acknowledge that your family dynamics are corrupted; you are being undermined as you 'dealt' with things and climbed all hurdles and mountains; you don't need to be subdued or undermined by that energetic realisation. Question to the universe - 'Let's see what we can do to help you?'

Me-' OK, (tuning with my hands, into their right shoulder) I can see you standing strong and secure in your passions, you know yourself, your mission, your creativity, your passion, yet this one element needs reworking. We need to take flight with an 'opportunity'. It's complex as it needs a physical shift of dynamic to restore balance; it will be one person, one person only that can reach you. I see now, it's your partner, he is waiting for you, he knows you, you haven't come together yet but you have met. You are still caught, you need to be open to the new, the new opportunity but it's the only one that brings alignment, be patient. To help you we need to give you the confidence to believe in yourself, to overcome all, even he misunderstood you. Be patient, real love is coming to you, he realises he can support you in your mission and there is deep understanding. Do not worry, be ready to shift, be ready for your lifestyle and life to change. Allow change in, you protect yourself from others a little too much. It's your way of stability, but the nature of your shift means you need to 'allow' someone else to see you, so it is important you let yourself integrate with another's lifestyle. It is different from yours, but don't worry, the two will become compatible and integrate, be open to the possibilities.'

There is then a sense of hope that washes through the sitter, but this hope isn't 'false winged'; it is genuine and there to enable them to receive and let change in. There is stability and security in finding a new path of enlightened understanding that feeds into the left shoulder as we touch in on heart and long-term vision. The long-term vision refers to lifestyle. I will break down this area further in explanation as it's very important.

Collaborating Energies

In the diagram we can see pencil lines showing coils interacting, from the heart chakra (green circle in chest) the pencil coil from opportunities (left) around the head into 'creativity in lifestyle' which literally means; creating a lifestyle.

The words 'partnership' and 'relationship' are connected to two slightly different areas, as 'partner' in a stable form operates from the centre of the heart chakra in the chest. The 'issues' around relationship are in the vertical oval that is split into three layers. The different energies of the three layers are like a house with a basement. The top layer being a first floor, with a view of clarity, security and direction; the middle layer(ground floor)- unsettled, need and desire. The basement represents deception, a feeling of being closeted or hidden, deprivation and lack. So the energies refer to the sense of receiving love in abundance. There are various reasons why a person may struggle to live on the higher vibration of enlightened security; all the energies need ordering, acknowledging and adjustment. Tuning in to someones heart space means acknowledging all emotions and working through all pains, clearing the heart to a space of infinite flow in love energy. I connect in by looking with my fingers, as if tuning in to an emotional archeological dig. Each element of energy, block, interference needs clearing or energising until left with an open and trusting heart. The energy should then build up above the left shoulder of the person. The energies always guide into 'deliverance',

155

asking corrupting forces, pain and insecurity to leave, by pulling the energy out or asking any intrusive energies to go back to origin. When the heart energy flows freely, the

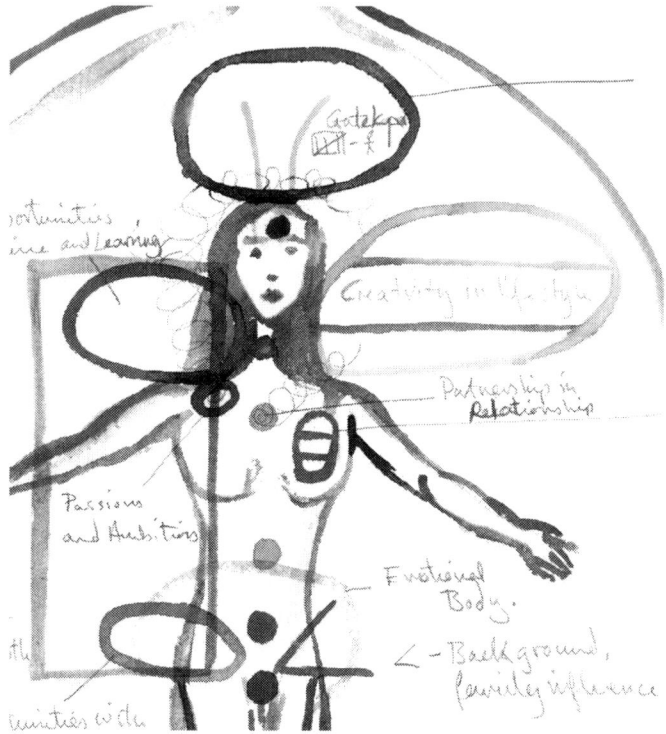

person can create their world from bliss, kindness, love, shared interests, understanding, security and dependability.

Seeing Partnership or Relationship

When I connect with two persons to identify the nature of their relationship, the energies guide my hands in different directions: when my fists come together as if symbolically holding the two people, I see them relating in totality. If they are experiencing clashes of interest, the energy tends to bounce off each other, so my fists collide. If the pathway is developing there is the sense of my fists moving forward as if representing two persons walking a life path together. The language you relate to in another's soul will communicate itself depending on your sensitivity, consciousness and state of awareness. The importance is tuning in and 'listening' to the person's energy. The energy will express itself in its own way.

Creativity in Lifestyle

You will see that creativity in lifestyle is split into three areas of interest in the yellow oval. The central position is in the balance of normal life; a consistent, loving and dependable place of creation. The area of blissful creation, is the section above, named as the angelic realm. This will not sustain consistently in itself, so creating from a place of growth, development, nourishment and nurture, allows a fertile growth and sustainable life, especially if the environment and relationships are all aligned with a generous sense of self-love. For you to attract in, those around you can ask,' How do I treat myself, how do I love myself? What do I do to create a deep sense of happiness and satisfaction in living?' Then look at how others treat you and see if there is a gap in your perception. Design your world around others caring for you as much as you care for yourself if not more.

Sometimes an understanding of how simplicity and silence leads to the active and profound manifestation of something beautiful, ephemeral and eternal can bring change; for instance, the sense of union, from a place of collective bliss, a feeling of being one. So instead of aiming for bliss we aim for love, sensitivity, honour and kindness. This in turn leads us to the bigger picture of a lifestyle profound and honest. The honesty is a true sense of living, authentically and from the heart, in which we know our security is founded on strong foundations, with values that enable a growth that sustains and gives us rewards and benefits beyond our expectations. We are able to expand on this by asking the universe, 'What else is possible to experience, to love or create with, to know?'

We have to be careful to clear any intolerances we have on the body or our sense of judgment on the self, as these are where we can get trapped in pain, guilt, insecurity, fear or lack. If there is any part of us struggling to accept ourselves we can let external energies torment us and interfere with our consciousness. Writing a list of judgments, intolerances and things we hate about ourselves, or don't like, can help to bring awareness. Clearing is by simply realising that it doesn't work to not love yourself, if you can love yourself deeply, you will attract love in, you will love others and you will share your 'understanding' of love with the world; you will be loved.

The Crown Chakra, Higher Consciousness and Gatekeeper

The Crown Chakra is the place of inspiration, light, bliss and enlightenment. It is where we can nourish ourselves and plug in to Source or energies that replenish our soul, enlighten, or give a sense of spirit or God consciousness; it is a place to 'feed' or receive from the universe. When functioning well, we can channel a limitless supply of energy, sense of love and inspiration, and trust in our intimate connection to the universe that all is love and one. But when this area goes wrong it can create havoc in the entire energy structure of the individual. The areas to look at in respect of caution are to do with the consequence of authorities of malpractice: if a parent or guardian has been inappropriate, been abusive or abandoned the individual when they were a child, there can be question over faith. If a parent has died, the person can feel abandoned also: if the community infrastructure of care or medical, legal, financial system has let the person down, the person can feel disconnected and marginalised.

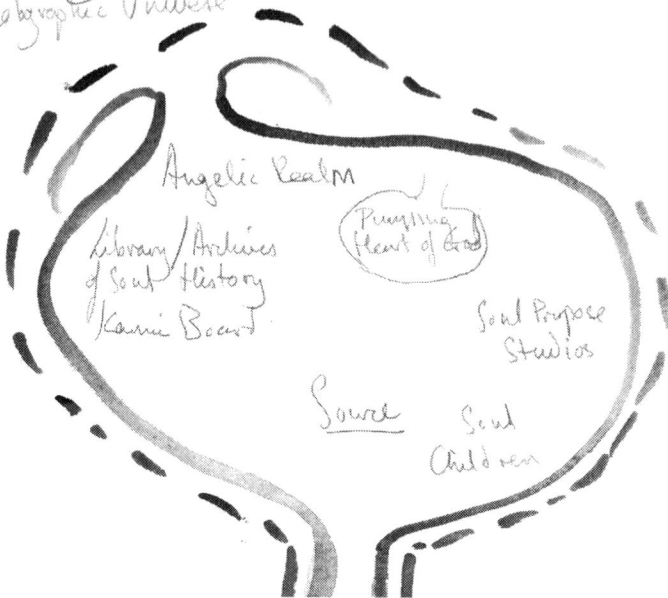

Gateway to the Void and 2D Matrix Holographic Universe

Angelic Realm

Library/Archives of Soul History Karmic Board

Pumping Heart of God

Soul Purpose Studios

Source

Soul Children

This sense of loss or disconnection can multiply in its confusion and chaos. If combined with an area of self-judgment, low self esteem, or intolerance, a person can start demonising themselves, allowing other corrupt and interfering energies to 'take over' their body. This means they may get angry easily, be destructive, deconstructive and have high levels of 'ego defence'; they may close down, or leave a discussion as they don't trust the process of resolution or the 'other' to understand perspective. Fear of not being understood, or not being heard, causes an insecurity and anxiety that a person feels they need protection around. They therefore disconnect and seek a path of safety in which they feel more comfortable and self-reliant. This can lead to them becoming a 'loner' or 'isolated'. The pain of loneliness is very real and life threatening, which can be made worst by the person letting in, in-authentic relationships and on a spiritual level much more serious; attachments, possessions and demons.

There are ways to clear these energies, but if the limited beliefs of low self-esteem cause the person to 'believe' they are not worthy of love, understanding, acceptance or presence, they can be programmed to accept 'less' than they should in their life. The higher conscious can therefore develop from a young age to believe that the person is only deserving of pain, abandonment, lack, loneliness, limit and corruption. Going on the journey of discovering which issues are most affecting the person, can take months. It's a long-term development strategy that often involves hypnotherapy. However by affirming 'I am amazing', 'I deserve love', 'the world is safe and friendly', 'I allow life to flow through me', 'my body deserves love', we start to allow gentleness and sensitivity in to the way we love ourselves. This gentleness allows us to start creating more far-reaching and limitless belief systems which serve us to expand our world rather than limit it.

We can anchor our higher conscious 'gatekeeper', at the gate of our Crown Chakra, to only allow beings that truly serve us from love, kindness and understanding to inter-relate with us. We can ask all other beings to go back to their origin, choosing a path of love, care, attention, acknowledgement and kindness. We may find some of the guidance we have been receiving, whilst in the most part appears helpful, in other areas, it weakens our aims. We need to feel sure of our possibilities and directions. If we find we are still attaching to any beings, we need to work out how we believe they are serving us. The limited belief that they are actually helping us, maybe due to a need for companionship and security.

There are many ways of clearing attached beings: ghosts, aliens, demons, entities, attachments. We have a right to our own sovereignty and our own body, but we do have to claim that right. We can ask all beings, attachments and demons to go back to their origin, to not bother us again or come back to our reality. If we struggle to let go, it is normally because there is an area of limiting belief or healing needed to bring detachment and flow to consciousness. To command or instruct them to leave, we can use the power of God, or our own sense of command. If we still hold onto them we have to ask ourselves how this being serves us. It can take time and patience to find out the contributing factors, often around an area of lack. They are often corrupting the life, mind, or a sense of body. Demon energies are very real and very corruptive, they can seem to threaten death and often carry suicidal messages to a person, making them believe that they are isolated and not able to be loved. This effort to create loneliness in a person's life is very destructive. They make the person feel a sense of separation instead of collective consciousness.

Delivery is through communion in collective consciousness; the heart of God and a reaffirmation that the soul is
connected to God; we are children of God and we have a
natural right to our sovereignty with God. Reclaiming the
body can take time and effort; sometimes it has to be
done on a hypnotherapy level. The true sense of God
love, housing of the body, collective consciousness and
light energy can restore balance. As 'sensitives' or 'medi-
ums' we may communicate with Angels, Buddhas,
Merlin, Demi Gods, Jesus/Yeshua, Archangels and other
beings such as Shakti and Shiva. The communications
take a bit of organisation and understanding. The priority
relationship is with the heart of God love, the heart of the
universe. This is the central anchor which is the factor
that enables all of life to co-create as one in love. The
other relationships, whilst often more tangible, are sometimes distractions and interventions from your relationship with God and can form corrupting forces in experiencing deep and true love. The vision of God is different
for all. For me, it's the heart of collective consciousness
and the doorway into the conscious universe.

**Clearing attached beings that limit our reality can be
helped by simple processes, we use natural laws to
make those processes easy and straightforward. We
have a right to sovereignty and exclusive use of our
body. We can use these 'rights' to let go of beings that
are attached to our soul or body, claim back authority
of ourselves, ascend in to our sovereignty and
command corrupting forces to leave us. To do this we
may need to acknowledge the complexity of pain,**

attachment, double bind, past life issues, oaths, promises or contracts, lessons learnt, understand our karma. We may also need to ask for the karmic board to re-generate our energies and give back anything that was considered a 'loss'. However, by affirming our rights of sovereignty and divine use of our body, we allow change and transformation in by simply asking the attached beings, entities, ghosts, aliens or demons to leave us.

When the energies are more stubborn, as with demons, or the attachment more complex due to double binds, a need to acknowledge past life history, karma, if there is a lot of pain, fear, or a void of darkness, I use methods to suit the needs of individual persons. The processes can be accelerated and found to be effective in combination with hypnotherapy, visualisation, energy work, meditation, emotional freedom technique, soul mapping, the sacred river of truth, clearing emotional black holes, demon feeding, the clearing of voids, or to integrate with a mixed healing approach. There are many different healing tools and practices that can be integrated effectively and built on constructively to help clear the energies and support detachment from low vibration channels of consciousness.

If there seems to be a difficulty in letting go, it is possible to look further in to the attachments of the beings -

- What do you gain from relating to this being?

The relationship is experienced with some form of reward; maybe companionship, security, strength, leadership, team work? Although the rewards seem accessible they normally compromise areas of living and lifestyle.

- Which part of yourself are you not allowing to be

loved? *There is always a limit to a relationship with an attached being, sometimes we see that the situation has created a protection around areas of pain, that are like deep wounds that are being hidden, it is natural to hide deep pain, this is an opportunity to bring light and healing to the experiences.*

- What lessons are you wanting to learn? After

looking at the complexity of pain, we always receive a reward through life lessons or values understood, we ask the question, what have I learnt? The journey in to this may mean going into past life regression, or looking at the emotional layering of pain, to see how deep the sense of pain is, pain has to be acknowledged to be released, the lessons learnt make it easier to move beyond the situation.

- What do you gain from remaining in a relation-

ship with this being? *The being serves the person, they may think they gain companionship, security, protection, strength etc. However the relationship is often limited by the nature of allowing the being to share the body and life story. By allowing ourselves to be under-*

mined in this way, by giving our power of life and living to another, we we start to reduce our state of sovereignty. We may in some cases not feel strong enough to turn the energy dynamic around, this is an illusion, by asserting that we want a one to one relationship with God, with sovereignty or by taking back our body we can ask the being to leave. We may have to release all contracts, oaths and promises with the being. By meditating on the complexity, we find the right pathway and bring release and detachment. We are then in a position to ask them to leave.

We then ask the universe for this to be cleared on all levels of reality, consciousness, ancestry, past, present and future, never to approach the persons reality, sense of being again.

We can then ask for any energy, values, or sense of self, identity, organs to be returned. We can ask for our needs in moving forward to be met and for the most benevolent outcome for ourselves to be served.

'I affirm I am a sovereign child of God, in a universe full of pure integral love, I deserve to be understood and loved in all that I am.'

With clear boundaries, supportive relationships, active understanding, it is possible to detach from non-serving relationships with beings that limit, undermine or corrupt. Eventually we find our world is full of loving and supportive people who allow the profound to exist in the everyday, creating magic and enchantment in our experience of unfolding awakening, uplifting our spirits to set us free.

Clearing demons is sometimes very complex; a journey of clearing deep pain. I have found that often demon energy manifests through emotional black holes or areas of extreme pain, insecurity or loneliness from a person's past. The energy centres often need healing before the demons can easily be sent away and a free-flowing consciousness can be attended to. Sometimes it is possible to feed the demon with the toxic energy of pain, body of pain, fear or insecurity; they then leave more easily. Often it is also possible to feed the demon the energy body associated with the root cause of the problem, this often comes through in past life work. There are many types of demon; allow healing to happen in its own time; by trusting in the journey of development and healing, you will bring resolution, listen to your feelings and needs the journey will develop naturally. The experience of feeling and experiencing entrapment by a demon can be frightening, isolating, however the pathway of healing will bring light, there is no need for fear, we can change the dynamics back as we claim our sovereignty and our relationship with God, as we move in to our mission and purpose; as we serve, their service comes to an end.

Invoke Archangel Michael to protect your energy. He will help with anxiety, sleeping and the path of light and healing. Archangel Michael is very powerful and available in the loneliest and darkest moments. Calling on Jesus or Yeshua to command demons to leave, can work to. Seeking to connect in to a high vibration energy of light to live through, can sustain disconnection, this can be topped up with energy healing sessions. These processes can also be worked through in hypnotherapy or visualisation. Sometimes, due to old wounds hypnotherapy is needed to seal the energy centre, to re-programme the conscious, clear black holes and to release the pain. Trust the journey and process in to resolution whichever path you take. Hypnotherapy can be a very helpful tool with these deeper bonds.

'I call on Archangel Michael to protect and guide me through my journey into light and deliverance to God'

Clearing Demons using Visualisation, Hypnotherapy or Trance work

Demons work for the Devil, they create oppression and a limited reality, the coping strategies to deal with that oppression or the emotions that create a sense of frustration or anger often lead us in to a sense of relationship beyond our nurtured path through passion or lust, oppression or rebellion. We may say or do things that are not contained within our value systems, we thereby feed our ego. The journey of clearing demons, supports the healing of childhood issues and deep pain. The journey of healing and resolution can feel overwhelming, feel life threatening and be totally exhausting. There are many different demons, here are examples of two:

• The demon Incubus(Male), is considered the husbandry or wife demon(Female-Succubus) as he or she attaches to the person as if married to them. The person then finds themselves shut out of relationship love and in a position of only attracting married or unavailable men or women. This arises through a number of different issues, maybe a past of abuse, sexual abuse, low self esteem or damage to the aura with a deep insecurity in the root chakra. Incubus, may spiritually rape, plant spiritual seeds or eggs within the women he attaches to. The babies eventually hatch and fly away. In the present day there is a lot of writing about Incubus and Succubus but when a person first experiences spiritual rape, it can be frightening. The process of healing is in clearing the person's rooted and deep pain of loneliness, insecurity, sexual abuse, low self esteem, or any death wishes.

• The demon Malphus is emotionally abusive. He governs the energy of a 'sensitive' being and terrorises them with anger and pain. The person feels unable to control their negative expression and emotions. The projections of the demons can cause the person to become abusive themselves.

Deliverance is achieved through many paths; however primarily understanding and release is given through the deliverance and commitment to God, or the heart of the conscious universe. The Holy Trinity of Sacred Father, Sacred Mother and Yeshua/Jesus(inner child) helps to give an architecture to this growth and development, with the strong powers of the universe insuring you are protected and held in a familiar love, this architecture insures your deliverance.

I pray to God the Sacred Father, Mother Mary - Earth Mother and Yeshua to be reborn in light and to be delivered in love, through the communion of my sacred family; as a child of the universe through the commitment to my path in divine will as I open my heart to the Sacred Holy Trinity, that they may serve me as I serve them. I open the channels of communication of giving and receiving and trust in my deliverance, Blessed Be.

Giving the demon the energy it wants can act as a way of releasing toxicity from the soul. The demon only attaches to low vibration energy, such as pain, fear or insecurity, so we can give these energy bodies to the demon. The body is organic and temporary and can be given away to the demon, enabling a re-birth similar to a baptism, in the process to enable a separation from demon energy, always finish in light in God's heart, what ever that means to you, then reconnecting to the body through re-birth enables the sacred temple of your own being to become your government through divine will.

Other ways of disconnecting through visualisation can be used, one method is to freeze the energy link with the demon. Healing the aura and black holes can be done through reprogramming the soul's matrix and bringing light in, closing avenues of darkness, soul mapping, this is an important unravelling. Be creative, the healing process is about clearing all emotional black holes, voids and deep pains so there is no room for demons to link in to the low vibration energy centers.

The last stage of healing is through accountability of the allowance that the demon was able to have entered the body, this also to be resolved, this thought form has to turn to light, we rebuild self esteem, re-create boundaries, realising the pathway of light has many gifts. We have to learn to trust the process of healing.

If you do not know the nature of the character of the demon, it is possible to ask what it wants, normally this is reasonably straightforward, then feed the demon the low vibration energy you have inside of pain, fear, insecurity and the pain body of the part of you that was locked in the soul drama attached to the pain. By feeding the demon you give them what they are attached to, you simultaneously detox yourself from the lower vibrations of pain, fear and insecurity, releasing yourself from the attachment to the soul drama. The demon should leave easily, on command.

Use your sovereignty to claim back energy and needs to help with your life and living through God and the karmic board. Trust that other beings are dealt with in their lessons and learning through universal consciousness. Allow yourself to simply nurture your connection and deliverance to sovereignty, the heart of the universe, God conscious but do ask for what you need energetically in healthy organs, finance, value, grace, wisdom, love, expansion.

The journey of resolution reconnects you with the external community to create communion, universal love and trust with God, The Holy Trinity and being 'One' with the world: Holy Communion.

Trickster

There are many tricksters; in sexual energies, spiritual beings and demon energies, these bring lessons around trust. However some also intend to interfere with your relationship with partners and with God. If we develop relationships with spiritual beings, we must remember the space we offer them and how that manifests out in the world perhaps as unavailability, distrust or as a 'relationship'. To define spiritual order, we need an 'order', hence 'logos'. I have learnt to assert that God is my primary commitment and relationship. Over a long journey spiritually, I discovered the only way to fully embody the heart of the universe and God was through this commitment. There will always be other spiritual beings to connect to: from Pan, Merlin, Shakti, Shiva, Archangel Michael, Archangel Raphael but to keep free of corruption and interference our primary relationship should be with God. The demons, ascended masters and angels do help us, serve us, guide us, give us aspects like protection, companionship, playfulness, they are 'of God', originating from the Creator, this should always be remembered, many bring strength, light, companionship or security.

There comes a time in our spiritual journey in which we need to step beyond the angels and light beings, to form a direct alliance with the heart of the universe in love, there comes a time when the order of the universe allows us to let go and move in to a more trusted space.

I therefore suggest questioning who you have resolved your primary relationship with? The commitment to God the Father will protect and serve you, the other beings will challenge you, support you, provide companionship but the union and the universal communion in love can be achieved through an active and honest relationship with God.

Addressing this order can help resolve relationship order in the physical world and with polyamorous relationships. Finding the understanding of the nature of your connection and how this serves on a universal level, gives a journey in to a trusted and committed primary relationship that is dependable, allow the universe to work this out for you, allow divine will to guide you into relationship. Trust in the oneness of creation, the heart, mind and body can be aligned and mirrored in truth when alliance and soul truth is sought.

6 ANATOMY OF CREATION

What is the anatomy of creation? Where do we look for resource and inspiration? How do these resources affect our creative expression?

The Higher Consciousness

The Higher Consciousness is the preferable place of inspiration, as it taps in to universal consciousness, divine understanding, wisdom, genius and the flow of creativity.

There are various exercises in catalysing your creative genius as follows: the mind's eye should focus about ten inches above the head. This area allows wise channelling of information, such as poetry and wisdom.

Automatic Writing

Poetry can be easily channelled by putting your mind's eye or focus above your head. The process can be helped by placing your left hand on top of your head(unless you are left handed), take an ink pen in your right hand: the sense of writing with the flow of ink should be with ease and a light hand in freedom of expression. Allow your mind to empty and concentrate on the area ten inches above your head. Allow any words or thoughts to be written on the paper in front of you, without thought or engagement. Do no judge what comes, simply write. Notice the rhythm of the energy of the writing and start to observe in an objectively conscious position, again without judgement, simply allowing the words to flow. When the energy stops, read what has been written, centring in on the essence of the words. Again take another piece of paper, and focus on this area of thought and wisdom, allowing the flow of communication to freely come through. Allow it to be prose, writing, poetry, gaining insight into the structure and essence of the wording. For examples please see 'Seeds of Light' by Amanda McGregor. Keep on developing your use of rhythm, wording and structure until you are happy that you are connecting into a bigger pool of thought.

Emotional Expression

Emotional expression is largely transitory in its objectives. It is a state of expression that bridges us into a much more whole environment. The reason being that it is often low vibration emotions (pain, fear, insecurity, anxiety) that block us from feeling the creative flow, oneness or enjoying collaboration. Gentle heart-centred emotional expression leads back into creative flow and unified connection of consciousness through expression of feelings. Feelings have to be acknowledged. Through this we are led into transformation, security and development. As long as we are heard or we self-validate our own inner sense of context to our feelings, we can move forward. Feeling the self-value of deserving to be heard through non-violent communication enables a secure platform of expression, connection and output, enabling delivery in vision and objectives. Emotional expression can be felt and connected to within and around the stomach area; emotions have to be acknowledged and validated, then it is possible to work out the complexity of thought patterns through discussion or breathing through the layers of the feelings. The complexity of emotions are experienced in the stomach area and are layered unless working with visualisation, past feelings or releasing emotional stress, then they may be stored in an organ. Emotions are often referred to organs relevant to the holistic significance, focusing the mind's eye on the organ whilst opening up to feeling the sensation within can help access the complexities, through feeling, visualisation, breathing. Breathing exercises that can be done to release or explore the depths and layers of emotions or The Sacred River of Truth as in A Life of Bliss can be used to unravel and release emotions.

What is Source?

Source is widely known as the heart of the universe, the consciousness of God, Heaven and Nirvana. It's the point in which when we are fully connected and present in a pure white light and loving energy; we are in a state of 'absolute'. My understanding and use of the word 'absolute', is in being fully connected in a multidimensional manner to 'true' experience and through this ultimate connection comes 'understanding' and a deep sense of 'knowing'. Once we have achieved a state of absolute we are well on the path of enlightenment. This state of absolute connection can be experienced by every cell in the human body, soul and in our innate being's relationship to the world and the universe. With it comes a deep state of peace due to the depth of understanding and enlightenment experienced through the whole journey of life. Source is visualised as pure white light loving energy. We can visualise a sphere of white light above our head and expand the energy to pour into us and embody us. We can breathe into the energy and activate our cells and expand the energy beyond our physical being into the environment around us. We can continue to build on the light energy until it connects with everything that is. We can breathe in the activating energy every day and allow the energy to heal us from any emotional hurdles we have, by breathing through our pains and confusions. When having a full orgasm this energy is tapped into, blissing us out. On an everyday level we can use meditation to enhance the Source energy and embody it, simply by visualising the white light sphere, pouring energy into us and activating our light bodies.

To develop the stages of enlightenment we need to understand the emotional self. This understanding generally lasts a lifetime. We have to remember if we are eternal beings there are a lot of emotions to sort through, however there are a few values that can help a person stay enlightened without trapping emotions further; unconditional love, non-judgement, forgiveness and heartfelt integrity.

When we are fully connected on a daily level we carry a deep knowing, or understanding; when we connect we experience peace, truth, warmth and love. This ultimate sense of reality can be experienced by an independent person and it allows ultimate independence, as this state of being is not relative to anything else.

Plug In

The easiest and quickest way to connect to Source is to do a meditation to 'breathe' open the chakras, by putting attention on each one, starting with the root chakra, seen here at the base of the spine, breathing into it, opening out in front and behind, then moving up to the sacral centre, breathing in front and behind, noticing the different vibrations, continuing up to the solar plexus, the heart chakra, the throat chakra, the brow chakra and then the crown.

Next, visualise a pillar of white light from a large sphere of white light above the head. The white light pours from the sphere into the top of the head, moving through the centre of the human body into the earth's centre and up to the top of the sky. At the top of the sky it is important to visualise a white starlight sphere similar in shape to a sun but white light.

Visualise this sphere opening up at the base and connecting with the pillar of light extending from the top of your head and allow this beautiful deep peaceful energy to ooze its way down the pillar of light and into your body: the energy brings peace, healing, wisdom and relaxation. Allow the energy to find its way all around your body slowly breathing it through, noticing how it relaxes all your muscles and emotions.

The Void

Beyond Source, the void is visualised in grey matter darkness as the matrix, the programme centre of the universe. It is beyond the light and love energy, as it is for practical intervention, in creating new possibilities and intervening with life for the benevolence of all. This is an advanced level of operation: to be in the void feels a little lonely and empty but the structures of programming are encouraging in creativity and programming. By travelling to the neck of a black hole in a trance-like state, it is possible to access a lot of data to help with intelligent constructs of information and reprogramming of life-activations and activities.

Creating a Vision

There is a difference between wanting something, receiving a vision and manifesting a dream. There are visions that are goal-based, mission-based, ego-based, value-based, emotionally motivated and projected. The best visions that are most likely to come to fruition arise from a place of 'inspired purpose' and community consciousness, which means they arrive from an external place of communion into the thoughts of a 'recipient', they attempt to take into account a wider community or culture and are for the benevolence of many. These come from a directive place of global consciousness, God consciousness and connect from your heart to God's heart or the universal body of consciousness.

Value based visions work well for small scale activities such as family life and small business. They embody the culture of activities and mission. When manifesting our dreams and visions we have to be careful of how much control we are taking in trying to make things happen. There should be a natural development process that picks up a certain velocity and energy, to enable doors to open and a sense of inspiration. A successful vision is often activated very quickly after it arrives in the sovereign's mind and is communicated out to persons. The persons, if inspired, will then catalyse further activity. The velocity of the development process picks up and very quickly there is a natural uplift and boost of energy that enables a sense of confidence that the vision is likely to manifest.

To make sure visions come from an inspired place it is possible to connect in with Source or a person's energy field. Bringing through visions for teams of people can be done by channelling straight from God/universal consciousness. This work takes a certain ability. There is a mediation process in collaboration, clearing hidden agendas and clarifying roles. Often a few pathways need clearing, values are assessed, priorities identified and rewards highlighted. An intuitive vision is also created for a strategy in financing, infrastructure, human resources and time frames of development phases. Then emergence is encouraged from an appropriate platform which enables delivery and communications. The platforms and market can also be identified through the vision.

To Create an Inspired Vision

Reach your hand upwards and visualise tuning in and connecting with 'Source' and focus your mind's eye in Source (as mentioned above). Then draw the energy to the earth, connecting the Source energy to the persons in the room and to your own being. Then hold a symbol or title of project in your mind's eye whilst tuning in to the energies of Source. Allow sensations to come forward in colours or symbols, welcoming in further information, or just asking for inspiration, allowing this information to build, sharing it with persons in the room. There must be an openness in bringing the information through as it allows an open receptive flow of energy. The more people engaged the more solid and obvious the vision. Then it is possible to ask questions about specifics and to go into further details about development phases, core elements of experience, product, objectives, roles and the delivery of objectives into manifestation.

Trance

Working with the state of consciousness gained from being in 'trance' has been recommended for centuries by 'shamans' and medicine people. Today we still use this intervention, however it is not considered so mainstream unless using hypnotherapy. Working with a patient, much can be achieved using trance; lets take a moment to look at the nature of the technique and the technology available by going in to this altered state of consciousness.

By stepping out of our body and allowing our higher consciousness to link in with the understanding or consciousness of the universe we can act as a medium for a greater power to work through us and catalyse healing and intelligence from a much grander source. We tap in to the inspiration from the universe, this can act through us to bring healing, intelligence and understanding.

In trance deep healing can be achieved as the programming is effective from the higher consciousness right through the whole system of psychology, the spiritual intelligence and emotional intelligence. We can attend to limiting belief systems, addictions, insecurities, major illness, depression and orientation, giving a person the confidence to become successful in their way. We can also open up to the universe and the revealing of the complications influencing and corrupting a persons psyche. They may have interference through sources not easy to identify or pain from a soul issue hard to locate on a normal level of consciousness.

Understanding another's reality and their experience of that reality is not up to us to judge; dealing with 'voices', divine interventions and experiences is a process of healing and understanding. A person experiences reality in a way that is 'real' to them, the sharing of this, is not for judgement. We can allowing the positive elements of their reality to find their direction, peace and the person to find strength in their well being. The direct relationship with the heart of the universe, collective consciousness or the 'God' consciousness enables a safe 'environment' to centre, in which 'belief' systems are exchanged for genius, profound healing, peace and safety in love.

Working with someone in the holding space of 'trance' allows us to experience the power of the universe in direct contact, feeling how able it is to adapt, heal, develop and bring peace. Creating environments of healing in trance enables a close relationship with an innovative approach that can transform and bring peace to people's realities on an magnificent scale. The space of trance allows us to experience other possibilities of healing and experience.

For instance with psychic surgery, hypnotherapy, past life regression, trance dance, creative expression and sound therapy. All methods of working in trance need safety and trained persons to 'hold space'. The exploration of these processes enables us to develop natural healing abilities to another level. The study of this area of experience has a lot of room for research, development and accountability. We are very un-evolved in the documentation and processing of the achievements in these processes; hence a very skeptical relationship with the scientific world.

Holding Space

When we lead a person or people on a journey of change we 'hold space'. When this is done effectively there is no room for doubt, insecurity, fear or anxiety. Leaders 'hold space' in many ways; through acting as a 'chairperson', teaching or development. We also can hold space for each other emotionally, physically and spiritually.

The two main components to encourage when holding space are unconditional love and non-judgement. These two aspects allow nurture, growth and encourage well-being in trust, safety, consistency and security.

By setting up a strong 'holding space' we can develop understandings and share intelligence or feelings to enable development, growth and nurture. This may be done through healing, therapy, intimacy, professional development or learning. We can then add values and inspired communications to encourage an uplifting experience; like banter or humour, whilst grounding with emotional understanding and holding space in non judgement and unconditional love.

Within the business and education systems these holding spaces often have a consciousness of judgement, however respecting opinions and enabling freedom of voice does not need to hold judgement. Discussion of opinions and ideas can simply be a rhetoric in creative thinking. This is about appropriateness and performance in inspired thinking; we can act as 'one body' in the development and flow of active listening and language to encourage high levels of production, activity and performance.

Helping a person get through their obstacles and reach their goals is about believing in them, the universe will do all it can to support that journey. Believing in a person encourages a strong supportive connection in which they feel held in a way that helps them to reach their goals. As soon as doubt or insecurity is projected onto a person, they will sink in to low performance or lack of self belief. They may even find new directions. This maybe appropriate but often it is simply a matter of perspective or working/learning style. How many goals did you reach when you had a partner, teacher, parent or employer believing in you? Self belief and believing in another makes a great difference to a person's performance levels. Check that you have a free flowing heart of self belief.

Belief Systems

We discover that we hold belief systems that limit our sense of reality and we have belief systems that expand our sense of reality. The process of healing and therapy enables us to explore those ones that hold us back and nurture those that move us forward. We may have formed belief systems from a very young age about the nature of our reality and the experience of that reality, such as the world being unsafe, objective, neglectful, too material or uncaring.

Working through belief systems often leads us to hold on to the beliefs that give us a limitless understanding of reality and let go of the one's that no longer serve us, we can use kinesiology with emotional freedom technique, hypnotherapy or other healing techniques to identify our belief systems and our relationship with reality. When we fundamentally 'believe' something we tend to create our life from this position.

Our sense of reality may include an understanding of subtle energies, voices of guidance, angels, God, the universal consciousness. If a person has 'real' experience of this expanded consciousness they are in their true nature not a belief system. Their reality is real to them. We must not judge another's sense of reality. However, belief systems can be limiting and lock us in to entrapped states of consciousness, belief systems are not always grounded in real experience. Limitless understanding around love and reality can encourage an open and non-judgemental attitude to compassion and understandings; we call this 'universal understanding'. Understanding a person's choices and their relationship to the universe based on their experiences, enables a respectful relationship.

Religion sometimes moves a person from a state of 'real experience' to a 'holding space' of defined spiritual practice. Unconditional love and non-judgement are not always understood and administered and some of the teachings are not always from a place of individual learned experience. We can understand and respect learning, values, spiritual relationships but we have to be careful taking on projections, limiting beliefs and judgements formed through some religious activity that restricts 'universal understanding' and limits our ability to compassionately love another without judgement.

Religion often has many values, learnings and philosophies that are valuable in today's world especially when the aspects of spirituality nurture a limitless peace and love through the integration, activation of spiritual intelligence, therapy and development. However sometimes the 'holding space' of religion can be misused and the teachings can project a distorted understanding of God consciousness, universal understanding and boundless love. By going on an inward journey to experience the universe from within we enable a real experience of spirituality, our soul and the collective consciousness which can activate our soul memory and open up the energies of infinite love and understanding. The real experience gained here can help us identify the role projections and limited beliefs have played a role in our lives, we can thereby enable a healthy and harmonised understanding of the way we spiritually relate.

Mindfulness

Mindfulness is obtained by emptying the head of thoughts and focusing on the heart. There are many talents that can be nurtured from mindfulness including the ability to focus, to be at peace, to come up with awesome ideas, to transform, to allow divine guidance in, to allow spiritual intelligence in, inspiration, to bring peace, to bring awareness. The main aspect that corrupts mindfulness is insecurity. Often this element is projected by an external party and can be dealt with through direct communications in making them aware of the position in which they are putting the individual and the impact. Insecurity is a massively corrupting force of creativity and project development so must be taken seriously. A person can energetically bring themselves to a position of security above the problem, by realising and celebrating their values, by enforcing their needs in respect of benevolence and a healthy outcome. Often problems are born out of ignorance or unhealthy competition; both are dealt with through communicating values, or essence of experience.

Artistic Processes in Creative Communication

<u>Painting with the Consciousness of Water</u>

Painting with the consciousness of water is a painting technique I developed, created through the combination of philosophy and science. Whilst creating a beautiful image it is possible to practice mindfulness and to empty the head of thoughts. The technique is very simple but very effective.

Whilst concentrating on the object being painted, with an empty head it is possible to allow the water on the paper to carry the intentions of colour and process through projection. The water finds its own image, through the colours injected into the stream. No pencils are used in this technique. The idea is to allow the water to carry paint and paint itself. The water holds the consciousness projected onto it; the colour that is injected in the water allows the content of image to manifest on the paper, through conducting intentional energy channelled onto the painting through the artist. It is a straightforward relationship, between the thoughts you carry, the water and colour palette in front of you. This technique is effective when one has an empty head, meditating on the object or flowers and when one uses water as the foundation, adding paint into the water content creates a photographic effect through image.

Abstract Painting

Abstract painting enables the expression of sensations, movement, change, spirituality or emotion, through the focus of the higher conscious and emotional space. To do abstract painting it is best to clear the head of all thoughts, then focus on sensations emotionally and from

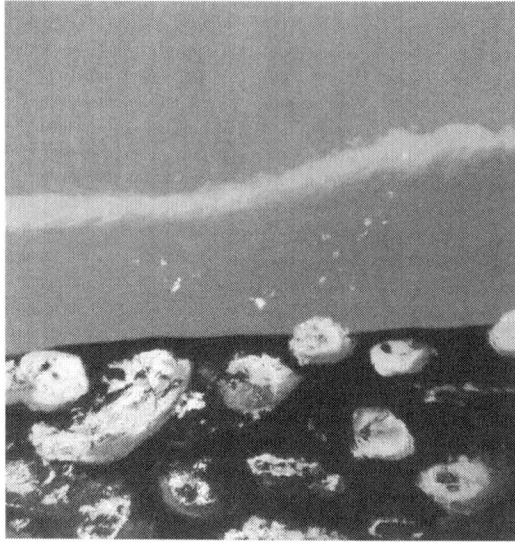

the higher consciousness. Getting into the energy of the experience takes us on a journey into understanding. The abstract painting 'Letting go' communicates to people in many different ways. Spend a moment reflecting on what the painting is about before reading on.

I wanted to express the experience of the digestion of heavy emotions that seemed to be like stones inside of me; the process of digestion took me into a lighter space of being; the process took me into light. Using a method of energy healing and meditation, the stones seemed to dissolve and become lighter, giving me the sensation of uplift or ascension. The coral, jade and golden colours, and gold, are symbolic to eastern spirituality, expressing a spiritual peace. The gold represents the alchemy of transformation, the sense of reaching a higher plane of consciousness.

Conceptualism

A concept is like an absolute. It is one sentence or a string of words that sums up the answer to a philosophical question and enables the space or manifestation, statement of truth, theory or debate. Conceptualism is very mindful. The process creates simple and effective 'products', art works, ideas with a consciousness very suited to branding, events, titles, science and creative processes. I feel the best concepts are aligned to philosophical understanding therefore they create a front like the tip of the iceberg that when dipped into, or fully explored encourages a wealth of understanding, scientific knowledge and process that can catalyse many inspired thoughts and directions to unfold. Just by changing the way we think about something we can become open to new perceptions that shine light on areas we hadn't been able to navigate or digest easily. The concept behind 'A Life of Bliss' which focuses on the root word 'org' hopes to encourage easy digestion into the anatomy of creation, development and communications, thereby enabling a foundation to encourage persons to develop collaboration, pathways, processes, creativity, products and services to suit the global community.

Channelling Paintings

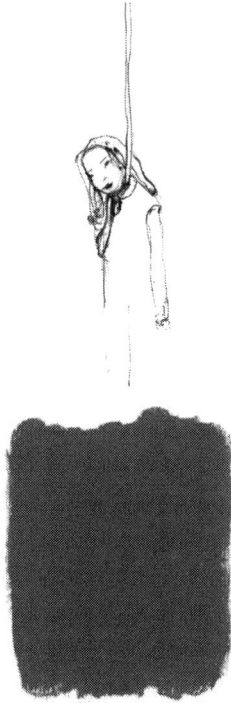

Channelled Paintings connect into the universal body of consciousness or collective consciousness. They can relate to past lives or past memories giving a sense of eternal life. They are held in the body and the higher consciousness. To express them takes a meditative process of embodying the character and feelings of the story; a bit like acting out a character from a film.

'In Memory of the Sensitives, 1600's', Image by Amanda McGregor

Divine Flow

Divine Flow refers to the energy of love, in its abundance from Source. This energy- frequency is a form of spiritual intelligence and can be understood to provide a place of understanding of 'God's Hand' in Creation. To tap into it, it's important to understand philosophy and how it influences the energy of spirituality. If science- based, it's important to understand how philosophy influences science and how spirituality influences philosophy. Spirituality allows for the experience of the different frequencies of energy that can channel through an individual in conscious experience; in guidance, intelligence, love, inspiration and nourishment. Philosophy allows for the universal body of consciousness to inspire working relationships into a sense of oneness, allowing presence and experience. Science allows for questions to be actively answered, development and growth to be nurtured and strives to seek evidence and understanding around philosophical and spiritual awareness.

To experience 'Divine Flow', as if aligning to God's mind eye. use a meditation to concentrate on white light, love, the heart of the universe, whilst asking for inspiration in creative or communicative needs. Spiritual intelligence is about using love and light in relating to and understanding the world to create a more peaceful reality. A lot of the work I do is creatively advanced, yet scientifically undiscovered. However, the results of these working processes are often highly successful, so when a state of awareness takes us beyond science and philosophy we

can develop concepts and communications, healing and therapy to enable development and growth without needing science to have evolved to the levels of these natural phenomena. Put your mind's eye in God's heart and allow channelled painting or writing to come through as if 'understanding God' in creation. This process works very well with inks.

Image - 'Hand of God', using black ink to paint and to build a relationship with the 'God Conscious'. Image by Amanda McGregor

Creative Processes in Communication

The Word

The strength of the word is empowered by authentic communication, from the heart and through to the core of our being. Words have power when they are said through intention, with truth, from a place of dependability or trust and from a place of divine will. Words have the power to empower, heal, or destroy so it is important to understand the use of words in safety and different forms of communication.

Historically, the intuitive people that were able to communicate with a strong and deep integrity mixed with an emotional and spiritual intelligence were persecuted and accused of witchcraft unless they were a priest or from a religious order.

Although there is now some historical respite, there is still little awareness around the nature of the historical threat that persons present when speaking words of universal soul truth. However there is an emerging under-standing that in the 'omnipresence' of the being that has evolved with their soul truth, their sense of reality, or universal presence seems to shine a light on those whom have not fully embraced their own soul or other intelli-gence systems, beyond the mind.

The way the intuitive's presence seems to reveal the limits in the less-developed person seems to trigger reac-tivity as the evolved person is seen as a threat: so a rebel-lion is formed through a want to silence, restrict, limit and sometimes kill. However there is always different talents, forms of genius, skill-set housed by persons, there is always the choice in which path to walk. I feel the intuitive should be understood for their own talent in their effective way; everyone has a choice in which path of development to choose and what form of intelligence to nurture.

The professional intuitive works for the benevolence of the collective so should not be seen as a threat. However there will always be persons in all industries that abuse their position and power. A genuine intuitive, whom works from universal truth is generally a very valuable asset to the world as a whole.

Historically, holistic persons helped people, had natural healing gifts and were persons whom were deeply attuned to the universe. They were the wise people, the medicine persons, the community leaders, the midwives, the sacred prostitutes (a spiritual sex therapist) and the herbalists whom in history helped others through understanding the ways, the rhythms and the matrix of the universe.

The complex history still has left a large mark in society, we still notice a marginalisation in the way persons who are are sensitive, holistic, emotionally and spiritually developed are related to in community. However in the United Kingdom a significant change happened when Churchill was in power as Prime Minister.

In 1944 Churchill began proceedings to change the aged 1735 witchcraft law, when his trusted psychic Helen Duncan was arrested for 'vagrancy' and 'conspiracy'. Churchill was furious and wrote a letter to the magistrate suggesting a waste of time in court with 'this absolute tomfoolery'. The case still went ahead and Helen Duncan served nine months in prison. However she was the last person in the United Kingdom to be accused under the Witchcraft Act. The Witchcraft Act was repealed some years later in 1951 to allow 'sensitives, psychics or intuitive's' to work professionally and for persons to develop their extra sensory perception.

Churchill himself made many decisions through intuition, he saved lives and steered the country out of war, he constantly worked with intuitive's and psychics and made many decisions using intuitive processes. The processes of remote viewing and channelling are especially powerful when working with development and strategy with worldly issues.

The role of development with the intuitive should be given a main stream position of direction, professionalism and placement in the community helping people with well being, health, integration, communication, unity, culture, organisation, developing the communities and countries in to secure and expansive futures.

If we think about this time frame, how recently in history things changed, the historical oppression still has an effect on persons that are intuitive and keeps the community and the 'sensitive' backward.

The spiritual or soul person often remembers their past lives; the persecution, the killing, burning, murder and hanging they experienced from the 1600's - 1900's, a developed soul will remember their soul history or be able to access their past lives, often they remember the significant nature of their relationships with other people through history. This 'memory' is sometimes hard to place logical understanding with, however the emotional experience expressed appears very real and takes time to heal from and to develop on from.

We are therefore still in a position of bringing development, integration and placement to intuitive's. We are now able to bring understanding, to encourage a supportive environment for intuitive's to manage, heal, develop, communicate and create. We are a changing global community.

Affirm: I support intuitive's in the community, my life and my relationships, intuitive's deserve to be seen, heard and understood.

Empowering the Elemental Creative Energies

We can call in the elements of Earth, Water, Wind and Fire when enabling magical transformation in nature and creativity. When in a magical circle of light, the ability to use the power of the 'word' is magnified.

We are in a place of trust in allowing our intuition to guide and inspiration to flow, when we 'command' our words hold power and give us a magical meaning in arriving at the deliverance of intentions. The words that come through this process have the ability to develop and heal. I wrote the following poem through automatic writing to encourage peaceful directions of Earth, Water, Wind and Fire:

The Elements

Earth, Water, Wind and Fire

The elements that inspire,

That humble and transpire.

We give the universe the power

To seek it's 'Will' and catalyse a 'Truth',

Amongst the hearts and souls of the people,

We seek truce.

We hold an image of a God, that allows a certain calm,

A surrendering of man, to abandon many of his plans,

To unravel his call,

And enable a Rule,

In the manifesting of a Heart,

We seek to inspire 'Divine Will';

The technology of Creation,

The matrix of the Earth,

A destiny that sparks,

Opening a gateway into freedom,

A bigger vision will transpire.

That settles all defence,

Giving a loving trust of heartfelt care,

To a community at large

In which all pain and deception becomes a grief,

A loss to the sea, a burial in the earth,

So we may ascend into the air,

Quenched with a thrill and a passionate will,

A fire that remains sure and burns forever in our hearts.

Non-violent communication

There are two elements needed for nonviolent communication.

- A connection with the heart

- Centered emotional intelligence in communication

The free vocal expression of, 'I feel….' is used to explain context to position, bring awareness, explain needs and boundaries and explain velocity of emotive, problem, interference or corruption. 'I just feel if we looked in this direction we would bring more understanding forward which would help us to capitalise on intentions.' 'I feel disappointed as you seemed to help yourself to that information. I don't feel you are acknowledging the work I have done, or the position I am in.' 'What do you feel happened there?'

Using questions to open up spaces of discussion can encourage calm and centred responses; so all details of the bigger picture are understood.

Speaking through the heart is achieved by imagining all the words you are speaking are dripping in love and directly being conversed through the heart space, this creates a loving cushioning in all that is said.

Trust

Trust is needed for collaborative experiences with other persons, the universe, the sense of journey, and flow. Trust is created through two elements -

- **Understanding** the true nature of an individual, environment or the universe.

- **Dependable** relationships with individuals, environment or the universe.

If either of these elements is interfered with, through a sense of insecurity, corruption, or a sense of lack, the collaboration cannot lead us on to create. Understanding and clarity in dependability is reached through empathy.

Empathy

Empathy is the process of putting yourself in another's shoes. Through this 'embodiment', we find our ability to understand another is wholesome, there is a sensitive and grounded knowledge of why they behave as they do. Through the process of understanding this holistically, empathy creates a deep bond, connection and helps us to find trust in another's true nature. This depth of understanding has the potential to connect us to another in deep love.

After a lot of work with people we can help with compassion fatigue through empathy. By moving from from a primary value of compassion to empathy we enable a process to allow love to inspire growth and development in a sustainable way, (without sacrifice to the self or others). Empathy also enables us to bridge holistic understanding, create healthy boundaries and understand another's omnipresence very simply, quickly and effectively.

Empathy is a very powerful tool that can bring peace to all sorts of relationships.

There are three techniques or tools to draw on with through empathy.

- When sitting opposite a person, exchange seats, then tune in to their presence as if wearing the aura they left on the seat. Explain to them the feelings that come up in being or embodying them.

- Use visualisation to perceive the true nature of a person's experience of living, by visualising a person in front of your clairvoyant vision, (imagine them about a foot high), take note of their characteristics, feelings, experience of being.

- Act as if you are the other person for a few minutes.

Needs

Our needs are fundamental to our experience of living, they are the aspects that enable us to function, live out our mission and feel our expectations are being met in healthy relationship. Healthy boundaries enable our needs to be understood as a foundation to the process to living. Becoming aware of being taken advantage of, exploited or taken on a ride helps us to recognise the boundary of when needs move in to a more self advantageous position.

The discussion of needs can be experienced with trust or security when a person is fully understood or has been in a position of vulnerability and has needs in moving past that experience. Talking through boundaries and vulnerabilities in being understood within the context of needs helps to acknowledge the importance of those foundations.

• Needs often relate to archetypal identity

• There is often a need to relate to those that inspire and catalyse growth

• Needs have to be met in physical aspects that enable the journey of living to function well; like access to water, food, a home, a computer, a car, a cooker, love.

• Needs have physical aspects that enable working processes to function effectively. Like tools to carry out our job, our lifestyle, our care of ourselves and each other. Needs can be energetic, through a recognition of important aspects in healthy living and lifestyle; like allowing love in, creating intimacy, support through emotional hurdles.

Communicating our needs can enable us to be effective, efficient and relate in sensitivity, empathy and love.

Boundaries

Healthy boundaries are recognised when the emotional pendulum of experience is calculated in a happy position. When feelings move in to a more anxious state, or insecure state then normally a boundary has been crossed. When there are feelings of undermining, complication, feeling trodden on, let down, disappointment, anxiety we find these emotions act as indicator that something may be out of alignment. We then look at why there are aspects of relationship and activity not functioning effectively.

In intimate relationship it is important to be able recognise boundaries from a place of giving and receiving; acknowledging different virtual spaces of experiences, giving understanding to intentions, gifts, rewards, needs and outcomes. So that a common understanding of experience and direction can be reached. If a person projects, bullies, has expectations in ways that are compromising or takes more than they should, an introspection is needed and a formal conversation about functional relationship, needs and strategy in moving forward is required.

If the person has problems hearing the severity of the problem, the relationship can break down as the invasion for the other person can be too stressful. Understanding the architecture of someone's boundaries is very important, if approaching that understanding with love and trust intimate relationship is often formed in a sustainable way allowing time and space to regenerate, transform and heal any hurdles when moving through fear, complication or insecurity. If giving space to navigate and change boundaries, affirm 'all is well', so as to not self sabotage a situation under going changing circumstance.

There is often a temptation is to push others away, that are invasive to boundaries, this may create space but it also may cause a loss of trust, so more importantly check that the person can actively hear you. If they can hear, boundaries can be created and asserted.

If they can't it is important to use distance to enable healthy experiences of living. Loving from a distance or on neutral territory can be effective for family members that are prone to self centred behaviour.

Understanding consequences and impact of ones actions through empathy can help to understand defence and transform situations to love.

Death

Death is a transformational, metamorphosis state of being. Creativity and death operate on two sides of the same coin; birth and death have similar juxtapositions. When we experience death in our lives we go through an extreme level of change, these changes often move us into a different position in our lives, the experiences bring new pathways and new opportunities for creativity and lifestyle. Death serves us to create new beginnings, new states of beings and new opportunities, we are at the mercy of the universe in understanding how small we are and how vast and powerful the universe is when going through these extreme states of change.

When healing from grief, becoming aware of consistency in life and the concept of death, helps release the stress of the unknown, the sense of emptiness and the possibility of relating beyond death helps to bring life to the under-standing of 'death'. When working with grief, I feel it is important to enable a relationship with the person that has passed beyond death. This can be done by-

- Communication through channelling

- Mediumship

- Visualisation

The relationship enables the energy of love to flow as a two way experience. When in communication there is often a way of bringing proof of the identity of the soul that has passed, the being is able to then give a sense of guidance for the person on earth, they are able to bring understanding to the person on earth. The being that has died can take the person on a journey to give an introduction into their new world of Heaven, Spirit or Nirvana. Visualisation enables the source of light and creation to be seen, life learnings to be shared and inspiration in new direction to be given. An atheist in life tends to be an atheist in death, they don't always want to communicate. Sometimes they can be surprised and adapt, other times they remain silent, we create our reality even in this moment.

When we end a relationship or we loose something significant in our physical lives; like a job, a person, a body part, a house, or a car; space is created to enable a new project, relationship or experience. Our journeys unfold, our fate unwinds, we are on the path of our destiny constantly moving towards our destination. Staying open to our purpose and mission from a heart centred position enables us to trust our unfolding and express our feelings and experiences with an open heart.

Confronting Death

The confrontation of ones mortality can be very scary. We are so connected and attached to the physical world, that the thought of being without physicality can lead us to look at an emptiness, that sometimes seems like an abyss. Slowly over time our thoughts are driven inward, our beliefs our reviewed and our understanding of 'spirit' re-aligned with. The questions that dominate us, no matter how strong we are, or how spiritual or religious -

• Is there life after death?

• Do I remain an individual?

• Is there a God?

• Will I be able to communicate with my loved ones?

To deal with these questions and insecurities I invite in the possibility of immortality, no matter where one is with one's beliefs, there is nothing to loose by simply playing with the idea of spiritual immortality. I suggest inviting the questioning through allowing in an experience: If there is such a state of reality as spiritual immortality how would that influence me and my state of understanding? Something beyond nothing has to be more appealing than an abyss of emptiness. So I suggest a focus on allowing one's soul to dominate the governing system of the body, mind and spirit; by inviting the mind to take a step back.

Allowing the soul to become the central intelligent system of one's being, enables a connection with the spiritual, energetic universe; a connection with all that is. The rewards can be enormous, connecting with the matrix of life, creation and the frequencies of divine presence;

angels, archangels, spiritual beings, ascended masters and the presence of God. The peace of relating to Source, the energies of love and light, enables a calm approach to the inevitable passing. Helping loved ones by sending energy, heart warming love, Reiki, really helps with ascension. Communicating to spirit and through the frequencies of spirit gives comfort. Calling on angels, ascended masters and a communion with God adds deep value to the experience of living.

Often healing and comfort is given remotely. I have many times helped family members bring comfort to their loved ones passing, by holding space through giving Healing Energy, Spiritual Energy or Reiki the person passing and by communicating to the family through being there, text message and phone calls. It is good to be able to hold space for the family and help guide them through the process by helping the person who is passing by giving them Reiki or spiritual healing so that their ascension is directly in to Heaven, Source, Nirvana, God's garden, in to the light. If the trauma or pain of dying was extreme, supporting the soul with healing is definitely helpful and needed.

The soul of the person passing needs to feel at peace and that they deserve to live in light and love eternally. So we can activate their soul to a state of light and blissful peace as they leave the exhaustion of their fight and their body behind. The commitment or deliverance to God, is technically achieved by giving healing energy of peace, love and acceptance in the intensely deep loving vibrations of God consciousness. By returning the being to God the Father. The reason for the deliverance and the committal is to help with a direct path beyond any interference of demons, possessions, attachments or aliens. I am saying this to explain that there is a technical purpose in delivery. Once the being or loved one has ascended they often go with the archangels and the family and friends that have met them on the other side, to reconnect with their vibration at source, they may take a while to recover energetically as souls but are often re-energised in heaven/nirvana/ source, so at some point they will be ready to communicate through mediumship, if beliefs and values allow this form of relationship.

Prayers during Ascension- Psalm 23

The Lord's my Shepherd,

I'll not want.

He makes me down to lie

In pastures green; He leadeth me

The quiet waters by.

My soul He doth restore again;

And me to walk doth make

Within the paths of righteousness,

Even for His own Name's sake.

Yea, though I walk in death's dark vale,

Yet will I fear no ill;

For Thou art with me; and Thy rod

And staff my comfort still.

My table Thou hast furnishèd

In presence of my foes;

My head Thou dost with oil anoint,

And my cup overflows.

Goodness and mercy all my life

Shall surely follow me;

And in God's house forevermore

My dwelling place shall be.

The Lord's Prayer

Our Father, which art in heaven,

Hallowed be thy Name.

Thy Kingdom come.

Thy will be done in earth,

As it is in heaven.

Give us this day our daily bread.

And forgive us our trespasses,

As we forgive them that trespass against us.

And lead us not into temptation,

But deliver us from evil.

For thine is the kingdom,

The power, and the glory,

For ever and ever.

Amen.   Matthew 6:9-13

Relating to Ascended Masters, Archangels and God

A sensitive or intuitive normally has a very special relationship with the spiritual world in which they receive love, guidance, support and healing. Learning the art of mediumship allows the communications and relationships to extend beyond the physical in to the abstract world of Spirit. There are different techniques in communications and healing such as trance, channelling and Shamanic journeying. All of these techniques allow an intimate experience of living with the core experience of divine understanding, collective consciousness and a move from the ego in to a state of oneness. The primary values to focus on are love and light; the more we open our hearts, the further our journey of experience leads us to a centered position of understanding in the core infrastructure of the conscious universe. The more we relate to the core of this conscious experience, the more we are actively heard and our needs understood.

Meditate on - 'My Father's house has many rooms'

What does this statement mean to you? How do you visualise the rooms, or the experience of living in a wholly conscious universe?

Connecting with the Archangels and Ascended Masters

The archangels are powerful beings of light and love whom provide guidance, protection, inspiration and direction. I work with the following Ascended Masters and Archangels especially but I will see which ones comes to me, this depends on whom I am helping, I set the intention for the relationship and healing through God:

- **Archangel Michael** is a strong being of infinite support, protection and effective guidance. Call on him to help you sleep, protect you from interference and corruption. Work with healing, lightness and boundary issues.

- **Saint Germain** is a powerful ascended master, healer, wise man and alchemist. He has a strong history going back to 1700 said to be very present during the age of Aquarius the earthly time frame we are living in, a deconstruction phase said to have started in 2012 to last

25 years, which will take us in to the Golden Age. This reconstruction of living is also a sustainable construction of worldly aspects such as new economic awareness, banking, development, communications and human technology.

- **Jesus or Yeshua** is the manifestation of God in human form, having lived on earth he is very well known. He has a strong ability to heal. Jesus can command demons or interference and corruption to leave. He can help inspire development in the face of political unrest, dictatorship, he can inspire new economic infrastructure and to heal from abandonment, torture and bullying. He helps understand dominance and submission and the surrendering to God or the collective with trust and understanding. Jesus holds space for sexual healing and inspires transformation in the self and relationships when working with Mary Magdalene. Primarily, I work with Jesus to help with ascension, commanding the devil and demons to leave and to help heal major illness.

Working with the three beings we create the three fold heart, the power of healing through the heart of God. The heart is symbolised through a purple(violet), blue(white) and yellow(golden) flame woven together in strength and power.

I anchor my primary relationship with God, the central communication system to the universe, I then

217

act through love, communication and healing through the three flame heart; to empower, heal and develop, allowing 'Creation' to flow through me and the persons I am working with.

Shakti and **Shiva** can be called on for balance in relationships, sexuality and harmony in female and male energies.

Merlin for joy, magic, wisdom and understanding. Merlin is supportive in clearing demons or interference and living lightly.

Books for further reading can be found at the back of 'A Life of Bliss'.

Using Philosophy to Create

Philosophy lives with the question; philosophical debate aims to create a journey of wonder in allowing the experience of living to be brought in to a more motivated avenue of discovery in experience and advancement. Philosophy allows consciousness to play a role in creative discussion and to have a place within science, giving a space of awareness to elements of living that are not proved by science, there-by giving space to create. Giving space for creation before a substantial formula or equation or formal discovery is in place, we have to remember a new creation comes before or in advancement of scientific discovery and even proof. For instance we can be conscious that the brain uses energy waves as a vessel of communication internally, yet we haven't measured the waves in a way to formalise the language. We are aware that channelled energy of love is effective to our well-being, our bliss and our experience of life, relationship and love making, yet science cannot formalise or explain that experience through quantifying the frequency of energy or the amount of that type of energy. We know there is a quality of energy experienced in different emotions, or speech, we can assess that our neurological and nervous system is constructive in creating neurological pathways for the senses to tap into philosophical understanding, collective consciousness and universal body of consciousness, yet we have very little evidence to define the structure of how philosophy and science create a partnership of advancement. Philosophy therefore has an important position in motivating science, in allowing exploration into these unknown territories of understanding, by simply asking the question, 'How is it we can experience these different emotional energetic frequencies?' We start a journey of discovery that may become a journey into science and into a formal understanding of how the nervous system, the neurological system and the senses connect and enable the communications of collective consciousness and global community to manifest.

Asking the right questions

Remember the universe is conscious, 'we just need to ask the right questions', we can access an understanding of the nature of everything. Questioning is an artful way of uncovering and manifestation. Questioning should be a form of focus, getting into the roots of the situation and the essence of the experience. We do this from an internal sense of interrogation or outward communion with the universe. Questions are layered and the process of asking can be different every time. I listen to my inner voice from the centre of my chest and go on a journey of discovery. If the project is at the early stage of development we can ask the universe. By putting questions 'out there' we manifest receiving ideas and direction.

What am I trying to achieve?

Who will this help?

What values am I looking to express?

How will I create a communication system that is engaging?

How will this carry content?

How does this inspire?

How does this catalyse thought and engage in high-level experience?

What is the nature of those experiences?

How can we enhance experience?

How can we create an element of luxury?

How can we gain feedback?

How can we create lasting relationships?

How can these relationships grow?

What architecture of information is needed to create access to these communications?

How does this technology or pathway expand?

How can this be financially sustainable?

What is the growth potential?

How can the experience be developed and encouraged over the years?

How can we expand on collaboration, nurture and nourishment?

How can we share new creative avenues of thought?

How can we expand and create access to global communities?

What is needed to sustain growth and expansion?

How can we make this bigger than we know?

Using Science to Create

Science is the foundation from which to build new discoveries and new advancement. By nature science creates, science and nature evolve, transform and enter new states of being. Science is creation and creation is science. Science provides communication, methods of engagement and understanding for already established models of natural creation, man made products and communications.

Over the years I have researched the neurological system, the nervous system and the senses. The senses are a gateway to a much bigger understanding of man, oneness and consciousness. But how does our intuition operate through our senses to enable positive messages, carried by neurons, and how do we communicate and connect beyond our sense of individualism?

The beauty of theories is that they are valid as ideas. They are valid as concepts and as possibilities to expand on the nature of understanding our experience of being human. Theories do not have to be right: as a concept, a theory is fully acceptable, simply as a possibility.

I have a theory that our senses operate through our neurological system like a radio. The messages are carried in an electrically excited cell, a neuron that transmits information through chemical or electrical signals. These therefore are catalysts, and possibly operate through different energetic frequencies of information. It is my understanding that it is possible to tune in to another's neurological system remotely through the senses. I theorise this is possible due to energy being a transferable system of exchange and connection. The engagement process means we can overlay our tuning system into another by simply overlaying the tool base, by focusing our mind and neurological system on another. By enabling our neurological system to overlay another person's, when we connect we have tuned in to the other person's system through our senses.

An axon and a dendrite, the components of the neurological tree that grows from the nervous system, are messaging systems. The energy signals are not always connected directly to receptors; there is a quantity of energy that charges with velocity, as the neurons send out signals, waiting for a receiver to connect and catalyse reaction. It may be possible to tune a foreign receptor in to receiving, in the more complex parts of neuroscience. To me it seems more than possible that this delicate technological tuning and radio system could be enabled remotely in a more wholesome way into the collective consciousness of man, enabling the science of communications, to signal and receive in a much wider and far reaching nature. This in turn would mean our senses could connect us to any person we choose to tune in to and could build up energy through communications and through experience. We can also embrace a psychology of unity, a way of connecting to all as we realise the central energy system of catalyst, universal consciousness.

When we start to realise how easy it is to connect to each other through our senses and through collective consciousness, we start to realise how important the nature of that energetic awareness is. That we need to feel uplifted to fully experience the sense of euphoric engagement, we may choose to engage in the most positively conscious energy system that we can experience, love and light, just as we experience through positive people and the blissful experience of orgasm. This sense of surrender to bliss is a neurological state of being manifested by highly charged energy catalysts that combine two people, engaging through sensory experience and sensory perception to build energy into unity and a sense of engagement and bonding. The electric charges are carried on pathways of ions with components of sodium, potassium, chloride, and calcium; the nourishment of these elements supports strong sensory perception and experience.

We can see the importance of philosophy, science and creativity and how psychology informs internal communication systems and when aligned with philosophy how far- reaching that can be; the expression of creativity and connection to unite us as a global community. Being able to work with this universal understanding of greatness, enables awesome experiences, far-reaching privileges. Keeping the energy high and on a free-flowing level of bliss and by combining philosophy, science and psychology we are in a position of creativity, in which we can motivate inspiration and communicate to a global community.

Organisation 4- An entity, institution or association that has a collective goal and is linked to an external environment. The word is derived from organon, its ergon, which means 'organ'. There are legal organisations, public, governmental, political, criminal and voluntary. Resistance movements can also be thought of as organisations.

7 CREATIVE PROCESSES IN DEVELOPMENT, COLLABORATION AND COMMUNICATION

Creating a Flow in the Bliss of Creation

Give freedom and allowance to involvement: working with 'trusted persons' who enable a surrender and emotional peace, so as to form collaborative relationships with clear boundaries, roles and assertive direction and communications.

Create an inner platform of self-assurance or security in emergence; a foundation for creativity, growth and manifestation of ideas. Align with physical platforms to enable emergence and launch of products, service or ideas.

Source origin of inspiration, in presence at Source, mission, communications, purpose, streamlining creative activity, anchored understanding of presence.

Spread/spawn seeds of inspiration for incubation by clearly communicating visions, objectives and ideas.

Observe and nurture the start- up process. (In time, let go of ideas/products/services/persons that do not function, sustain or allow growth.)

Stay in presence, sustaining growth with inner value and outer product development, creating strong intimate rela- tionships, which allow inspired creative thinking and dependability in delivery and manifestation.

Surrender to bliss, giving yourself to each other without control, resistance or ego: creative collaboration in oneness. This is a commitment to integration and finding direction in divine will: Allowing 'universal will' to give an open pathway.

Create expressive and expansive communications with platforms that distribute and communicate into collective/global consciousness.

Nurture and Nourish

Sustain growth and expansion, by allowing a gentle and loving approach to communications and growth through a deep connection with the global community; active understanding of needs and experience through dependable persons, strong connection with product or service product and delivery through expansive distribution.

Creative Process in Internal Development, Collaboration and Communications

- Set up the environment for development process, by raising energy, meditation, humour, connection, sharing, and emotional intimacy. Initiate confidence, team building, activities, fun, non- judgement and open conversations. People merge into a collective position through deep eye contact, open understanding, connecting, feeling accepted, emotional bonding, making light of possible clashes.

- Outline project, product or service objectives or goals.

- Outline areas that the product or service brings resolution, enables support or is useful.

- Looking for root of the message in the product or service; in semiotics, experience, creative experience, journey or essence.

- Look for the nature of communion. How the communications and product or services bring a sense of unified agreement and benevolence to the intended community. (How resolution and solution arrives or is delivered to give a higher quality to lifestyle or experience)

- Ask the collective and self for a symbolically creative vision of imagined outcome, in nature of service, product or experience.

Internal Communications

- Share the different visions of team members.

- Using the shared information to integrate collective consciousness to streamline pathways and clarify emotive, rewards, inspiration, benefits, nature of interests, motivations, connections and opportunities of growth.

- Agree on working values or open book policies, confidence, acceptance. Identifying weaknesses and strengths.

- Checking team members are a seamless fit in collaboration processes. If there is someone who does not 'fit' the team, they will need individual development or to be delegated to another area.

- Develop roles and individual pathways.

- Assess investment energy of team members from perspective of money, relationship, time, hard work, travel, experience.

- Assess inspired rewards due to passion, growth, challenge, natural pathways.

- Nourish talent through a deeply supportive environment and nurture person's needs, to allow project delivery with dependability.

Finding your Bliss

Passions	Needs	Objectives

What do you need to work with every day, to enjoy the inspiration of living? If you could look back at your life and be happy with who you are what would you achieve?

Which values do you need to work with in your daily

life? e.g. - love, dependability, ease, money, happiness, communication, humour, design, creativity, light, connection, concept, intimacy, colour, transformation, evolution? etc.

Life	Business/Work	Relationships

Which values do you see appearing in all columns? If you could streamline your ideals in to one sentence, which values 'call' out to you? Finish the following:

For instance:

My passion is the 'creative spirit'

My mission is in allowing the creative spirit to touch, heal, evolve and create.

My vision is to bring enhanced processes of development to the global community.

My ideal colleague or clients are entrepreneurs, sensitives, intuitive's, creatives, leaders, people in development or communications. The next page is blank for your notes.

My Passion/Love is

My Mission is

My Vision is

My Ideal Colleague or Client:

How do I recognise Self Sacrifice when following my Passion in Business and Creativity?

Allowing ourselves to be motivated by our 'passions' can be rewarding in creating our direction and future but unhealthy when in the start-up period as we can be a little compromising to our values, through relationship, rewards of finance, ideal project, ideal client. We may need extra funds or work experience to fuel our path, so we may settle for an aspect in which there is a reward but it is for the sake of a part of ourselves or our values. We may take more from certain investors or supportive people than we want, or 'prostitute' ourselves a little by compassionately giving without a sense of sustainability in nurture or nourishment. This behavior can also reveal a crevice further down the path when in crisis.

The problem is that these coping strategies can stay with the development of the project right through causing a 'pulling down' or energy burnout from empowering situations that are a little too limited through their own dysfunction. Fueling projects that are unlikely to make full fertility for the sake of monies here and there, can create a short term solution with a long term problem. Be careful to ask, 'Which parts of myself am I self-sacrificing to enable this project to launch?' Cleaning up, is about re-inventing boundaries and values. 'Has this person my best interests at heart?', 'Are we in service to each other for integral reasons?' Going through this clearing enables us to claim back integrity and exposure of needs and vulnerabilities so as to compete in a healthy and open way with the global market.

How do we remain away from the ego and from attachments to power?

Power structures inform an individual's priorities and cause. Those that work with sovereignty, whom give their government to God or collective conscious, rely on divine will for decision making processes. Often in life when an individual is not attuned to nature or the universe or the God conscious, superficial aspirations of power are put in place through status, politics, wealth, legal binds and sometimes bullying or dictatorship. The life lessons attached to abuse of power happen whether a person is in command of their destiny or not. The universe seeks to bring us out of our ego and into our hearts through a path of realisation that shines a light on compassion and kindness through understanding and dependability, a trusted security that serves in non material gain, and serves in benevolence to all, this communion is set to care, nurture and find a growth in living that satisfies and rewards. The power play of disempowerment to empowerment crosses back and forth through its dominant and submissive elements until a person finds balance away from the ego and with a centre of heartfelt communication that is non - violent and energising.

Often when we enter into a state of awakening, kundalini rising, attunement with the universe or universal consciousness; in which our head fills up with the universal body of consciousness, the spirit energies, the Christ consciousness, we seem to become the creators of destiny: the God head, the wealthy entrepreneurs, the healers, the lovers of life. Yet this tremendous power confuses us as to which pathway to take, how to help the world, how to relate to others. Over time we are forced to find grounding and to enter back into our presence, source our mission or purpose. We find ourselves in truth and with the will of 'inspired direction' guiding. We realise all this energy is not us, it is in fact the universal presence of the God power or oneness channelled through us. We are ourselves quite impotent; we have just found a plug-in of power. Learning new ways of communication that enables a humble dialogue that encourages feelings to be aired and distances to be bridged, taking away from a head filled with illusions of power. The awakened person is often newly in a state in which they can 'bridge' all. They can see the world as one, and they lose a need to be an individual as long as supported in their mission and purpose. They are a part of a much larger 'organism' or organisation: the universe. The breakdown of separation allows a surrendering to divine will. Over the years we learn to not control but to gently catalyse and lovingly nurture, nourish and develop others. We fertilise, prune and weed, enabling healthy growth and a strong sense of destiny and destination. Our inner environment arrives at a place of functional and healthy growth which is represented in worldly achievements; it is mirrored in technology, social science and movements in consciousness. A Life of Bliss emerges to allow a light pathway of diamond energy, raising awareness and consciousness beyond lower vibrational forces of corruption and interference.

The ego has to be acknowledged and integrated. When another appears to say something that feels disempowering, it can feel appropriate to self-empower and self-validate due to anxiety, pain, a feeling of being misunderstood and a sense of insecurity. However this can appear arrogant and defensive. Communicating to another how their actions or words made you feel disempowered, sharing the boundaries of when you felt supported to when you felt undermined or not heard can start a journey into integration. Often our defence systems operate too quickly on impact of an obtrusive moment. However, it is normally possible to explain post reaction and reactivity to the sensitive nature of the territory they have trodden on. Re-connecting with the bigger picture and love shared, enables a grounded communication around processes and understanding. Re-activity and defence can be very unbalanced and unreal. Grounding with a centre of love combined with the use of empathy brings perspective and calms down defence systems. Try to stay open to the journey of understanding and learning.

When another seems to be a threat to personal circumstance, to their sense of harmony or control or their personal environment, they may find their entire system can close down and block another, withdrawal or push them away, or fall out of love. This reflex can be magnified to the circumstance or true nature of the conversation: we call it reactivity. The ego can instruct a sense of limited belief that the environment needs to be controlled to keep balance and a sense of security. This often communicates from a place of survival. If another person brings wants, desires, questions or demands to challenge that idea of personal space, environment and balance, the experience or conversation can feel threatening. Conversations are places of change, of challenge, or creative possibility, they involve two persons; one of those persons may not have all the facts, understandings, or be in a position to know how to relate in that moment, give conversation space to be understood. Ego defence can be very destructive. It is the trigger of close down and radical doubt in which all trust leaves the person and they choose to isolate themselves rather than trust the journey of communication, change or the allowance of possibility. They put themselves in a safe place away from the potential of being hurt, even though the hurt hasn't normally actually happened. This form of resistance is very present in therapy, hypnotherapy, love relationships or when authorities challenge a person to come forward with information or be present. The radical doubt, or insecurity in trust, or sense of loss of control has to be dealt with on a very deep level. Making choices that enable a trust in a choice of the pathway due to a sense that the experience is likely to be filled with light, to be expansive, to be a stable place of growth and an open pathway, enables connection and trust in connecting to new environments and people, enabling new opportunities for connection to be ventured in to.

Often these adjustments have to be made on a hypnotherapy/higher conscious level, the ego can can be very controlling and protective over its 'territory of control'. The affirmation, that you can communicate and have the skills to share your needs, wants and implement visions should be asserted.

'I am actively heard, seen and cared for, in my feelings and ideas.'Repeating this again and again can restore trust. The affirmation has to go into the higher conscious to enable programming right through the system of consciousness.

There are occasions when relationships cannot function because no matter how many times you explain your feelings, the person doesn't seem to hear. This is normally because there is a loss of trust or an underlying agenda the other person is attached to. This agenda may be a priority above you, which will mean there is a certain level of futility in relating or expecting movement in those areas. Adjustment, awareness or distance is sometimes needed if this is so. A healthy relationship recognises boundaries, underlying agendas and shares presence through quality of time and benevolence for all persons involved. Looking for pathways that allow all persons to be happy, validated and valued can enable a complex set of circumstances to find direction.

Non judgement allows space to connect in with feelings and understanding, to allow communications to take place beyond ego. The problem with defensiveness is that it is a breeding ground for judgement which stirs unrest and chaos in communications. Steering well clear of judging statements, and behavior patterns allows relationships to form their own path, with a grounded context, enabling a straightforward path of communication to unfold. To break through defensiveness always ground with, 'How did you feel about (that)? or 'I think I need to hear the bigger picture? What happened?' etc...

Ego can be important in understanding value in not being exploited, used or taken advantage of, but instead of defence it's a good idea to assert boundaries and acknowledge the context of expectations and needs in reference or relationship to the situation unfolding.

For instance, 'I can offer you a day's work, however I would appreciate my travel expenses included in the fee. 'Or 'I am feeling a little spent as I have been traveling this month consistently. I am more than happy to offer you a consultation but could you please consider coming to me?', 'I feel that since you are making an extra one million on this deal, I would like you to consider giving me a reward here? What kind of figure do you think is appropriate? Let's see what feels right?' 'Yes, I can offer you (this) in respect to the value of opportunity you have shared.' 'I was fine with the way things have been going over the last three months but now I feel we have changed direction and my skills are being used in a way that I was not expecting. Can we talk about this? I am not as inspired with the opportunities as they present. We may need to manage things differently', 'Were you expecting (this) to be so?' What resources have we got?'

So offering a lot of questions for the person to think out and being clear about boundaries, to do with time, energy, or skill set can be helpful in explaining the circumstance and changes in processes and how that in turn can affect us. Of course this kind of communication around boundaries can be helpful in asserting needs and avoiding feeling undermined. Asserting statements directly to a person should really be gentle and from the heart.

If talking isn't going to bring a decision and the pressure is on, so there is a need to speak out and make a decision independently, it is best to explain the velocity of the problem as quickly as possible and guide with an assertive direction of how you want to move forward so as to limit damages:

- I really feel unhappy about the way you are managing this. I need us to take a step back and re-think the problem.

- Please do not enter the meeting room, it may disturb the development process for you to go in.

- I feel you cannot hear me, so I need to ask you to to take a step back. I am serious.

- I have enjoyed working with you in collaboration: I will do my best to make sure we can carry on with the project without interference.

- I feel you are allowing us to be interrupted. Could we please seek to reduce interference on our meetings and our relationship?

- I am observing that this man is not very open and I would not normally do business with him. I would prefer we took a risk-free approach and carried on looking further a-field for a new pathway.

- There are elements in each other that we are struggling to accept, so for now we must spend time understanding how to relate safely.

- I feel you have offered me the minimum, but I was of the understanding we had a deal at 50%. I would like you to take on the responsibility of this decision to share the 50% profits. Will you be able to honour our agreement and resolve this?

Talking about sensitive problems to another can be done by sandwiching two positives around a negative:

- I really enjoyed reading your summary, but we need to check in with the style of writing. The content was really inspiring though.

- There is huge value in your points at meetings, however we really need to present in a cleaner style, I think there are many options for us to consider.

- You know I love you, but you seem to always let me down when I need you. However I know we will work things out.

The ego protects from love as often the heart has lost trust with the journey of connecting and surrendering from past experience. The heart defence can often be mistaken for ego and seems blocked from love. However an overly protected heart can recognise love and seeks to reconnect in trust. Distractions in lightness, humour, activity, dedicated focus can help to alleviate these defensive aspirations enabling a joining and union in the development of an honourable relationship and pathway of light.

15) How do we remain present, allowing spontaneity and intuitive process, whilst practicing mindfulness in our daily lives?

The flow and journey of working with unravelling processes should be allowed to be nourished and 'protected', as the pathway or journey of everyday life is like an energy flow in which opportunities, inspiration, connections and objectives are adhered to. The energy has to remain strong and in a state of 'free spirit'. There are many interfering situations that can crop up to stop the constructive energy flow, so we need to allow for change and flexibility in day-to-day life. All meetings and connections need to give a sense of constructive exchange and spontaneity, whether they are playful or serious. Presentation, pitches and speeches must allow for deep intimate connections with the persons and audience, allowing humour, closeness and familiarity. To enable intuition and spontaneity in presence it is important to factor in these environmental needs, giving space to persons having their personal needs met, in finding inspiration, in connecting to the collective and being able to feel their way through their day in arranging a meeting or creating a concept. By living in the moment it is possible to co-create in alignment with the collective, allowing a global sense of creation through communications, product and services. The environment needs to be designed for life, living in the moment, be highly flexible and be connected to platforms that allow large crowds, audiences or communication channels for connection, engagement or involvement. Allowing this level of spontaneity, connection in presence and adaptability allows a prosperous, innovative sense of flight that gives wings to the most sturdy of operations.

8 Using Intuition for development and Communications in Business

The questions I am asked in consultation around business development are mainly about investment monies, business models, infrastructure, strategy, mission, product, communications, market, fits for collaboration, partnership, team members and growth pathways for individuals. These are followed by development pathways and the clearing of outcomes for delivery into long-term vision. Teaching a person to 'have vision' is a philosophical journey of understanding, in which the collective consciousness has to be acknowledged, and the ability to find sight and inner communication needs activation. Depending on the individual, it can take a series of development sessions to bring a person fully into vision, into their intuitive understanding and internal communications. This then is naturally integrated with their working processes, performance, expression and communications.

Intuitive questions are often asked to the self, me or the universe whilst developing a business project or business. These questions can be asked in a meditative state, such as The Sacred River of Truth, or they can be tuned into with the senses using visual symbols or names to represent the objectives, company or organisation, in remote viewing, or kinesiology. Often it helps to do the exercises with a partner, colleague or friend, allowing a state of gentle presence and connection in to the true nature of the circumstance. Always go into the process with a completely open mind and empty the head of all thoughts, ready to be in communication with the conscious universe, listening and feeling intently.

Will I find investment money for this project? How long will it take to gain?

How do I see the development of the business?

What is the best internal infrastructure of this company? What is its pathway?

Will we get the investment from this 'named' company?

Pitching - What about my work makes me feel passionate?

Elevator - What inspires me about this working process?

Rooting Around - Getting to the bottom of things or sourcing the roots of the project, branding, communications, emotive, needs, using creative processes to inspire communications.

Further Questions:

What architecture of information do we need?

How can we develop the branding?

How do I see this 'named' person collaborating with the team?

Do I see this idea/vision/business succeeding?

Which areas do I need to work on to give this business the right foundations?

What is the most effective method of communication about the product?

What is the most effective channel of distribution?

Can I identify the strengths and weaknesses in team dynamics to help with human resources? What do I need to understand in respect to partner collaboration?

Do I think this (product/service) will be a hit?

Will we work with this 'named' company?

Will I have a good experience of this project development?

We have a problem with the way these two characters play off each other in the (collaboration). Do I have any further thoughts, inspiration?

Does this (name), work as the (title/branding)?

Will this (music/image) work to brand the (experience of the product/service)? What adjustments need to be made?

What is the pathway of this (product/service) company?

What do I need to know about operations and my role?

Will a merge with this partnership run smoothly? What are the focuses with change management?

What is the style of this product? What is its essence? What is it's purpose? How can I inspire a magical sense to it?

Communicating to your Market

We can use creative communications to raise awareness of the product and service product through a creative expression of the essence of the experience of the product. This can be achieved by developing an understanding of the presence, characteristic or aura of the product. This helps us to create a style to the experience in communications, packaging and branding through the development of a strong image. We can create this characteristic through a development of the understanding of our message, our mission and our values: we then give the product or experience a voice.

What does this object or experience want to say to the market, the world, people?

Why does it deserve to be heard, experienced and seen?

What story does it want to create if we were to breath life in to it?

What journey of distribution would we want to give it?

How do we want the market or the world to experience or integrate with it?

What communication is needed to build up an understanding around the evolution of this development structure?

The constitution of the business should remain anchored as the foundations of all product development.

By looking at the characteristic of the business products and service products and the essence that we would like to communicate and relate to, with our market in mind, we can develop a sophisticated story of experience with raised awareness, messages and learning. Sharing how the product or service adds to quality of life, brings resolution, development or value in experience, we can mimic the nature of that understanding through artistic means, humour or a developed understanding of the benefits the products or service bring. This area of development can be a lot of fun, bringing a feeling of bliss, social experience, shared understanding, saturation, solution, vividness and engagement.

Using the different forms of creativity mentioned in the previous chapter combined with a deep understanding of the market and methods of understanding helps to build dependable creative relationships that enable a global community.

The social platforms enable an interactive response, that encourages creative work to become viral and enhances relationships with the products or experience. The building of the relationships secures the longevity of service, the sharing of genius and the more far reaching mission of the development strategy. Looking at objectives from a far reaching position enables the product to serve to the highest potential. Allowing engagement in creative freedom of expression encourages a bonding and liberation, in which the self serving relationships created through the product serve in a unifying an dedicated way, enabling the product or service to have a journey and a limitless life span.

Different types of Consultancy

- **Directive** - When direction is given directly due to an intuitive understanding of the bigger picture and circumstance. Although grounded with the present, there is a 'sense' of future in timescale and likely outcome.

- **Advisory** - When advice is given through an intuitive glance at options and by asking questions about possible pathways, with guidance and advice around a higher level of probability in one or another outcome.

- **Mentor** - The meaning of mentoring was derived from classical Greek times; someone who imparts wisdom and shares knowledge with a less experienced colleague, enabling an intuitive approach into the individual's own wisdom and a shared understanding of imparted wisdom from the experienced intuitive.

- **Coaching** - When questions are asked in respect to goals or highest priority outcomes; staying in the present.

- **Therapy** - Intuitive approaches of therapy can provide a sensitive understanding of the whole person. Intuitive therapy connects very deeply to the person and reaches them; energy healing can restore a sense of well-being and nourish the person. Insecurity, fears and pains are cleared or acknowledged and the highest priority intentions are worked on to enable outcomes, uplift and direction. With a therapeutic approach, the past of the individual is acknowledged in respect to present hurdles, to help a person move forward.

Intuitive practice allows for all these types of consultancy in one meeting, enabling external factors to be acknowledged when sourcing direction, enabling a 'realistic' approach to an individual's growth, journey and development.

Active listening and understanding gives a thorough overview of the individual; their talents, passions and mission, and helps to align into the lifestyle they want through an uplifting and empowered approach of creating reality in the enabling of nourishing and nurturing projects, lifestyles, relationships and dreams. They are working towards a secure, prosperous, loving and understanding sense of blissful living.

Different types of Entrepreneurism

Creative Entrepreneur - They tends to be sensitive, make decisions through intuition, creative products or services, often small scale but when multiplying products can become large scale.

Social Entrepreneur - Often the entrepreneur will come up with business ideas that take in to account the welfare of the community, they have strong visions that can make the environment healthy, bring economic flow to the community and create jobs. Often intuitively inspired.

Small Business Entrepreneurship - Self Employed persons or persons that have a dream in running a life-style business, often vocation based and operate in functional ways to small business.

Scalable Startup Entrepreneurship - When a person has a vision or an idea that can change the world and they know the world will engage in that process and business. Often intuitively inspired.

Large Company Entrepreneurship - When a product or service scales into mass business, the company will go through cycles, trends and expansion, they may need to be hyper adaptable to meet the challenge of changes in technology and communication, however the products and services have a resilience.

Intra-preneur - An entrepreneur whom operates within an organisation or company to expand on opportunity, product, development, direction and communications. They influence and inspire the company to flourish.

Legal entities for entrepreneurs to create business structure. Please research the below models, to find the most appropriate for you -

Limited Liability Company

Sole Proprietorship

Limited Liability Partnership

General Partnership

C Corporation

S Corporation

(Benefit Corporation)

The architecture of the company structure should allow for agreements, operations, obligations and expectations to be creatively and expressively defined with order, space for expansion, sustainability and a limitless expanded understanding of success.

There should be a constitution to anchor the company in values, mission and ethics and an understood process in handling disagreements such as mediation, options for development and sophisticated communications with boundaries and needs understood.

When deciding which model of company structure to work with, we can ask the following questions?

- How am I protected, if anyone I am working with wants to leave the company or stop working with me? Is there an exit strategy?

- How am I protected if sued? Is there unlimited liability?

- How much tax do I pay and how is the company taxed? Am I personally taxed or is the company taxed? How many tax forms have to be filled in?

- How public do I need this company to be?

- How much flexibility or adaptability do I need? Which aspects of my company need flexibility and spontaneity?

- Does the ownership of the company need to be flexible? Is there a distinction between the board, directors, shareholders, managers and owners?

- Will the directors, shareholders, board all agree on values, constitution, mission and the process of conflict resolution?

- How loosely do I need to place operations with a partner? Or how tightly do I want to act in partnership?

- How much will it cost to set up my company? Are there any on going charges? Are there any on going processes that I need to uphold, like board meetings? **Investment** - We can use intuition to look at pathways and outcomes of investment strategy, portfolios or funding strategies through remote viewing, by tuning in to the energy through a symbolic way of identifying project or secured interests, shares or profits. Remote viewing helps to find constructive pathways, clear areas of interference and secure interests. People have different skills with intuition with stocks, shares and numbers.

A few Options for Intuitive's with Charging

Fees - Off the shelf, I.P. by the hour, encouraged through promotional experiences that enable easy access to taste the experience, allowing a flexibility and spontaneous working structure.

Consultancy - Quality of Experience, monthly payments to the intuitive through a retainer, in the journey and catalysts of that journey, through presence, development, creativity, communications, commitment to highest priority intentions, delivery of projects, vision, solutions, opportunities and goals.

Budgets - Person or business centred? What is your budget for this? Over what time scale?

Value - Self Value, or business value, in how the person relates to money and how much value they can share in experience. How much do you value the services? The product? How much would you be willing to give financially in respect? Assessing value is made accessible through an active understanding of inspiration, limits and boundaries.

Product - Percentage of value added after product expenses; value of experience of use of product.

Contract - Through a company or project based contract. Enables security and commitment, contracts create an effective working structure in companies and projects that fully accept the working processes of the intuitive. Often intuitive managers and entrepreneurs work effectively with contracts.

Organisation7 - An organised group of people with a particular purpose, such as a business or government department.
The quality of being systematic and efficient
The way in which elements in a whole are arranged
(Oxford dictionary)

9 CREATING A BLISSFUL LIFE

Inner Logos - Personal Self-Organisation

Relating to the world through our senses informs a different outcome in our relationships, pathways and journey of life. We make informed decisions based on a different set of information. A highly developed intuitive is called a 'sensitive'. The true journey of an entrepreneur is a sensitive business as the way a person relates to the world holistically is expressed through thought and action and deed. This means any blind spots or boundary issues also get projected out into the world. This can cause great hemorrhaging of wealth, or energy, as without a raised sense of consciousness a person can be relating to those who undermine, are trapped by contract, or appear manipulative or controlling. After about 15-20 years the entrepreneur often starts to become aware that his childhood is having an effect on his business decisions. We therefore go through a process of clarifying and 'ordering' the surrounding environment. This can lead to major life changing developments; divorce, changes in partnership, independence, sovereignty, court cases, tax issues and exposure of abuse and scandals.

I have worked on many case studies with the entrepreneur and a very similar set of tools is needed as the creative. When a person is independent in the world, on their own journey, they only have themselves to look for answers and decision-making processes. When a person is this independent they tend to have advanced leadership skills that encourage personal sovereignty. Personal sovereignty is a highly valuable pursuit, described as the relationship is with God and man directly; known philosophically as the universal body of consciousness.

The journey of 'personal self-organisation' involves the 'bridging' processing of feelings or emotions, the clarity of boundaries, the development of internal communication skills, the alignment of values with people and working processes and the alignment to true talent and destiny from a position of purpose; a true understanding of personal power and intuition. Most persons on their life journey are aware they are doing 60-80 percent right but that last part is really undermining their performance.

The sovereign often has a problem with confidence in the early stages of their life; sensitives are often misunderstood in their intelligence and find themselves undermined in partnership one way or another. The low self-esteem can create foundations of partnership at an earlier stage of life that doesn't serve at a later stage of life. The sovereign being, by nature is self-sufficient with their relationship with God and the global community. A healthy partnership, in both business and relationship should be inspiring, dependable and a vessel of growth.

Energies benefit wholly from a constructive understanding to the quality of experience in value and investment strategy, which means, all monies, energies and relationships should be able to add expansion of quality of experience in creating more. More time, energy, finance, lifestyle, home; an ease of flow in relation to responsibilities. Communication platforms and social networking sites should feel empowering and accessible, with very little corruption through adverts, exploitation and threat. The sites should be there to uplift and empower a sense of communication, as if drawing inspiration from the light, to keep a kind and sensitive way of development.

Taking care of the flow of energetic nourishment, means using everyday awareness of 'light' and supportive activities, such as drinking water high in mineral content, cleansing emotional energy with showers, oils or salts; eating organic food, sourced for seasonal needs; walking on earth or grounding to enable a download energetically into the earth.

Light embodied meditations, encourage the light body to sustain and to support abstract thinking. Meat eaters benefit from eating stress free organic meat from responsibly farmed animals. Eating into the Light is a book written by Doreen Virtue which explains different ways of nourishment when designing a light diet of nourishment. A diet that supports the neurological system and our senses should be high in sodium, potassium, chloride and calcium. For instance fruit, vegetables, nuts etc. It is important to properly research a diet that suits your individual and holistic needs.

Keeping our immune system strong and healthy is a good protection from most illnesses, however we are all vulnerable in many ways and when illness hits it can feel daunting.

The way the pharmaceutical companies are commercially structured and sell 'patented' drugs, to the healthcare system and 'general practice' with medicine can create some areas of disfunction. If you have a condition or diagnosis that seems untreatable or you want more options, always look further through research, to see what else is out there, as often the answers are easily reachable and on the internet. The pharmaceutical companies protect their territories through heavy patents, which can restrict and limit options. Always feel that you can research the exact nature of your illness and put together your own treatment plan, with the help of research, Dr's, holistic persons and nutrition.

There are many ways of encouraging a healthy immune system, here are a few-

- Natural yoghurt

- Soil Based Probiotics / Any Probiotics

- Caprylic Acid

- Charcoal

- Reiki

- Black Walnut Oil

- Clearing out fungus from the body (There are now products that help cleanse candida out of the body, by suppressing the cell wall of the chitin in the candida)

- Colloidal Silver

- Vitamins and Minerals

- Mineral Water

- Physical Exercise

- Juicing / Nutrition / Herbs

- Holistic Healing

- Emotional Freedom Technique

- Hypnotherapy

- Immunology

- Essential Oils

- Medicinal Love - Love that is of a deep and caring nature

Creating Life from Love

Filling your world up with compassionate kind people who are thoughtful, inspiring, intuitive and sensitive themselves, allows you to create a reality that channels and facilitates creation from a place of love and deep understanding, enabling a dependable and trusting environment to encourage a platform for living holistically that encourages expansion and growth into all areas of success. This gives us untold wealth in the experience of living, basing our relationships on experiential outcomes and quality of experience in inspired exchanges, time, energy and process.

Using Sensory Perception to enable a sense of quality of experience in living and working can be reached by aiming to create 'harmony' in all avenues of experience, thought and communications.

- In the uplift of light, pure and comfortable smells.

- The sounds of a beautiful voice, music, heartfelt, non-violent communication, teams of people that create high- energy in banter, inspiration or kindness.

- In tactile experience, texture, massage, closeness, hugs, intimacy or familiarity.

- In a visual sense of vivid colour and natural daylight, using SAD lights; enabling a feeling of satisfaction in the experience of visual saturation that enables a true sense of creative experience through deep integrity of the layers of engagement and experience in concept, communications and harmony in vision.

By enabling a quality of experience in light, we start to create from a place of bliss, enabling a kind and loving environment, to allow a reality full of limitless possibilities and trusting relationships that inspire and add experience to the quality of living and working on earth.

To create a work or home environment that keeps us in the flow we need to nurture spontaneity, flexibility and release from contracts that limit and from people that don't serve. We need to be careful to not attach ourselves or anchor to one environment enabling a sense of growth that can be global. This can be achieved through on-line communication systems.

Intolerances

Intolerances can be understood and cleared by writing a list of the things that you find irritating about yourself, your character, your body, food, your partner, your life, your family, your environment; the most irritating or unacceptable aspects of life.

The process of acknowledging them, then looking for ways to create peace, acceptance, non-judgement, healing and digestion, can have a massive effect on improving the quality of your experience of life. Healing can be carried out through emotional freedom technique, kinesiology or the Sacred River of Truth. Digestive aspects can be both emotional and physical. We can be intolerant to certain foods and then discover there are certain people in our lives to whom we have an aversion; the two seem to sometimes have common elements. Managing the relationships or communicating the feelings and complications can help to heal from the intolerances, separating a past experience from the present and restructuring understanding around safety and security; can help to move past these problems. With intolerances of foods, it sometimes is a question of rebuilding the digestion system and upping the immune system, then healing from the allergies. If you have a serious allergy, don't take risks of trial and error in your healing process, take it very seriously.

When it is hard to fully be present in the body, due to severe emotional black holes, or a problem with loving the body, eating disorders can develop, the trust of allowing the body to operate smoothly can arrive through a 'trust' in life and food. It is important in these cases to eat organic food, or responsibly sourced food. The body can be very expressive in not wanting certain foods and sometimes it is important to re-educate a logical and common sense approach into trust. The ego defence here can be very destructive to a person and the intolerances can kill the person if not handled carefully. Surrendering to the knowledge of nutrition and trust in organic food is important in regaining a relationship with food. If the ego defence is too active and the intolerances are too large, hypnotherapy can sometimes be useful.

Other areas of intolerance for sensitive persons are:

- Un-natural lights, in computers, over headlights in airports and offices

- Noise pollution

- Foods

- Being touched in certain ways or perceiving the body in certain ways of intolerance

- Smells

- Sensing feelings in others

Clearing intolerances and areas of unacceptability helps us to love again. We may put in different boundaries, we may express different values, we may resolve our differences, but through understanding we can remain clear and consistent in how to keep the relationship nurtured and strong.

<u>What am I intolerant to?</u>

In Others?

Of my body?

In Myself?

In my Partner?

In my family?

In my line of work or business?

Which values do I want to operate with? Which part of myself do I need to listen to and value?

Will these parts/identities/values be understood?

What boundaries do I need to assert to remain in a healthy place of relationship, development and growth?

How can I express myself creatively and communicate the development of this journey?

How can I take back ownership of my reality, my body, my mind, my soul and my lifestyle?

Most of these areas can be healed through a development process of understanding, intervention, options and a clearance of intolerances. The frequencies, or pitch of sound or lighting, can be addressed through a therapeutic approach with an understanding of the different experiences of pitch or frequency, then the reintroduction after interventions are identified.

Sometimes it is possible to heal from sound or light problems by slowly introducing the intolerance into the system after understanding the whole history and nature of the intolerance through therapy. S.A.D. lights and natural daylight can be helpful to give the light needed on a deeper level. Often by using a coloured film with computers we can change the experience or a background colour can be used. This is the same for reading. The light can jump around on white paper which can interfere with reading books and music therefore many people use a coloured film to enable the experience of reading to be clear.

It is also possible to source the root problem of the intolerance of that frequency of sound. By understanding when the sound frequency was firstly obtrusive to your experience, we can then change the relationship to it. Of course not all areas of intolerance have to be healed from; sometimes it's a question of acknowledging and accepting it and then making the possibilities of experience more widely expansive, so not letting anything hold you back.

Affirm- 'Even though I can't sit in an office with an overhead lighting system, I can use a portable S.A.D. light to free me to live a normal life'

Affirm- 'Even though I find reading hard work, I will be patient with myself and use all tools available.'

Affirm- 'Even though there isn't enough daylight in my office I will talk to someone to arrange to be seated near a window.'

Affirm- 'Even though my body likes to digest foods that are organic and simple, I can be patient and healthy to my body and give support to my immune system and digestion system'

Affirm- 'Even though I prefer to not be around crowds of people, I know I love everyone unconditionally and as long as I easily feel able to love and accept them, it isn't tiring to be around them'.

Affirm- 'Even though I can't stand the smell of going into that shop, I know that the food they produce is responsibly sourced and so it is the natural smell of organic produce, which allows me to be present with it'.

The empath learns through psychic development not to tune in to others unless they need to or have permission to do so. The boundaries are the same as choosing whether or not to tune in to another; you either do or you don't. Many people complain about a sensation of being pulled down by other people, however learning to detach and not tune in can enable more freedom in relationship. If it's not possible to tune out due to the intimate nature of conversation, I find the best way forward is to acknowledge the painful emotions of the other and then take the relationship into a lighter place through digesting and processing them, through acknowledgement, then into humour or a positive outlook.

Affirm - **I am able to relate to the world positively, naturally and remain open with all my senses every day.**

Financial Matters

Becoming conscious of the banking system and the 'credit system' is important in understanding 'debt-free' culture and making informed decisions about investors and investment strategy. Spending time researching this area of interest can help to build a foundation of living that enables a lot more freedom in the end. Loans should always be low interest but to understand borrowing it's best to fully research 'Positive Money', a movement away from debt culture, to the accumulation of wealth through the understanding of building societies and banks that attempt to operate with less emphasis on debt and more on positive money and a positive constructive angle on wealth.

Other ways of dealing with finance are through gifting, self-build, inherited, nonprofit, exchange, trade, crowd funding, government funded. Finding conscious intuitive 'Angels' can help to create positive money for sourcing investment loans. There are inspiring, conscious, light persons in all walks of life; from solicitors, investors, brokers, architects, therapists, creatives and writers. The journey is all about finding those persons that act as beacons of light and building and creating your world around them. What would your world look like if it was filled with people who fully saw you and the value of your being? If they presented to you in an empowered and nurturing way, that nourished you into the full potential of your talents and ambitions?

Affirm - **I am able to have a conscious and elevated relationship to finance. I feel a free secure flow with wealth.**

Contracts

Contracts can bring security and serve, or they can be damaging and limiting. Contracts can take the forms of partnership, contract work, retainers, written aims, loans, investment deals, marriage, mortgages, job security, direct debits, development strategy etc.

We can also create contracts verbally, through agreement, promises or oaths. A contract should allow flexibility and a sense of understanding around creating from a place of lightness, so as to manage or avoid stress, limit, pressure, dysfunction or futility. A contract works to enable the original visions or goals to have the potential of becoming far more than expected, by enabling a sense of 'What else is possible?'. We create an environment that starts to enter a way of development that removes us from hanging on to expectations. Expectations can be dangerous in creating disappointments and dysfunction. Having agreed reasons to release or create clauses or exit strategies can help keep a flow and an allowance in a trust of light living, strong working processes, constructive building and enjoyment which means that if things aren't working both parties can agree on exiting. Putting routine meetings in when relationships become complex helps to create an architecture to communication that enables a constructive process or pathway to find new direction.

Checking all your direct debits regularly to ensure they still serve you keeps personal financial matters clean and appropriate. The same for those giving to you financially: check in with them to make sure the choice of having a contract serves to sustain and expand, in a flexible and secure way.

I feel it is important to not fear living with or without contracts, although in business there has to be a way of commitment to end intention. We can use our intuition to assess how much energy we have for a project or development phase and how strong we feel about the pathways aligning. We can introduce a certain level of adaptability in the way we create our contracts and in the way we intend to operate in a strong and direct manner of manifestation.

Affirm - **The contracts and agreements I operate through serve me to be free and secure.**

An Approach to Opening a Contract for an Intuitive

a) Services - The Consultant agrees to use their 'wisdom', 'know how' and 'intellectual property' to perform advisory services, provide instructions, guidance, development and related services to and for the Company in order to assist and support it to raise interests as (per the below options), with an active 'understanding' and 'listening' of the areas listed. The terms of Consultancy are in respect to value in presence, commitment to vision and highest priority intentions and quality of experience. The client agrees that the services of consultancy are provided for inspiration, clarity, catalysts and enhancing potential and performance. They are not based on evidence or fact.

The Terms of operation for the intuitive consultant are with the added values of flexibility, presence, spontaneity, allowance, creative dialogue, activities, communications, acceptance, stillness, honour, love, sensitivity, silence, non judgement, understanding, confidence of personnel and dependability.

Affirm - **I am free to design my contract, options and interests in a way that suits my growth, nurture and nourishment.**

Legal Issues

The way the world works means that on occasion there is a necessity to go to court, to deal with tax, legal issues, contract, divorce or assault etc. The court is a place of 'hearing'. When the court is effective, that 'hearing' is considered an active place of change into a new beginning or reality. Court can be very effective in this way if there is an understanding of how to relate to it or communicate when under its authority.

There is more than one legal system. The most commonly used legal system for personal issues is statutory law, however there is also common law, corporate law and maritime law etc. These legal systems all create a space of creative perspective in the history of law and how one person's rights are effective. There are ways of relating to law to enable you to re-claim your rights in all sorts of incidences, however to work with the understanding of how and why, it's important to raise your conscious awareness around the legal system.

To understand contracts and how legal papers interact, it is useful to research 'freeman' thinking and the 'natural sentient being', or the 'strawman'. Most of these papers and audio guides are available on the internet. They help to assess understanding with 'natural sentient being' rights and help to provide a position of relationship to law. Learning about our contracts with government, from our birth certificate, our passport, our relationships to banks, healthcare and tax, can be very helpful in understanding how we relate to the system. We can sometimes feel too burnt out from serving the economy, the government, a company or the system. By raising conscious awareness through the education of these systems of thought and contract we become a bit more knowledgeable in our rights as free men. There are different levels of appropriateness with the system for everyone. I choose to embrace the system from an empowered state of understanding and awareness, so that I feel more comfortable relating to it, however others choose to detach completely. We all find comfortable ways into our own sovereignty. The ultimate freedom is the right to self-govern through sovereignty, without restriction. This leads us to realise freedom is a myth; there is always a binding part in life that holds us to a committed response. However, we can lighten up our relationships with those commitments, through an understanding of the economy, the court system, education, tax and of options in how we relate to the world.

Affirm - **'I am empowered to use legal systems to encourage a healthy approach to living and lifestyle.'**

Presenting at Court

To understand court we have to understand the balance books of compensation and the need to prove, or work with evidence. The whole court system works around evidence and the number of persons willing to come forward and acknowledge the nature of things. The compensation factors are normally financial, but in today's experience there is an understanding of development through training and education in awareness in some areas of problem. The role of development in law and as an act of adjustment and intervention will get stronger over the years to come.

When presenting at court the system is designed to judge and to ensure that evidence and witness statements are concrete and of a high standing. The very nature of judgement normally causes a sensitive person to defend themselves instantly. Defence reactions may include:

- Avoiding the court hearing.

- Becoming reactive, judgmental, frustrated and defensive when questioned.

- Talking from the head instead of presenting openly from the heart and with emotional clarity.

- Nerves may cause a sense of mixing of words, even to a normally articulate person.

- Not being able to recall huge spaces of time, conversations and experiences when questioned.

- Judging the evidence or persons involved in the scenario/story before a judge or jury has decided how to relate to the information and assess their own judgement.

These problems arise as the defendant feels undermined. They are after all meant to be 'under the standing' of the judge, which means they are being fully asked to give all understanding to the judge in trust. This can feel like being bullied into false reality; however it is to enable the sharing of information. There is an area of inequality in this dynamic, which means the sensation of facing a judge can feel undermining and bring up issues to do with trust. I therefore teach the same communication system to enable an empowerment of the person as if talking to a bully. The communication is humble but shares the full velocity of the story and the effects of the situation on the person.

I encourage people to focus on the abstract sense of assessment, their emotional centre and how they feel about the situation, the persons involved or issues raised. This way of communication allows the possibility of demonstrating the velocity of the effects through sharing one's boundaries; the outcome and the unfolding experiences relating to the circumstance by giving a visual context and evidential context with communication leading out through inter-related experience communicated by how it 'seems' to be and how it 'feels' to be involved with the circumstance. As soon as a defendant moves into judgement they become vulnerable to attack through judgement on themselves - they become judged. So to keep a safe place in court it can be beneficial to allow a large emotional space of operation in how the circumstances are 'believed' to have played out. When there is little evidence, a person's case can be built on through experiential witnesses who have fully experienced the problems the complainant sets out. Recounting the story as the defendant or court witness felt it happened gives a concrete and open time frame of unfolding events or circumstance. This way of integrity opens up the defendant to being able to be honest and open whilst safely recounting the experience through sentences that start 'I feel... that the way... the situation seemed... etc.', always using a sense of abstract experience, no matter how complicated or how extreme. When fully re-living the moments, one tends to remember everything, every sensory detail, which creates a strong impact on the court and is a very empowered way of communication in handling the information shared.

Keeping in such a gentle position when then being cross questioned, enables an anchoring with the defendant's truth, so they can guide those listening when they 'feel' the questions are leading away from 'that's not how I feel things happened' or 'I do remember saying that to him', however 'I feel... the context was slightly different... from my perception... the underlying agenda here was.....' So by acknowledging the way the questions are aiming to expose and divert from the main issues, it is possible to contextualise. When a person is communicating gently, from the heart and openly, they rarely get shut down, as the consistency in which they bring information to court allows a full picture to be understood.

Preparing someone to present at court can take months of development, as all the psychological aspects have to process to create clarity and a natural, empowered response. Moving a client from victim to empowered person is all part of the journey. As the cases often take a while to gather evidence and to come together, this time is often used to prepare a person to take the stand. I find this work challenging but deeply satisfying as it enables a complicated system that often further victimises the defendant to operate in fairness. Feeling in control in how we communicate enables a tool set in creation that empowers us beyond those life hurdles that limit.

Using Remote Viewing at Court

Remote viewing is an intuitive process which can empower into a strategy of effective communication and presentation of evidence. Tuning in to an image of the court system and complaints raised we are able to assess the highest priority point needed to be supported in enabling a positive outcome for the defendant. Tuning in to the persons involved in the hearing (the court witnesses and the judge) and tuning in to the strength of the case, it is possible to identify security, response, limit, judgement and likely outcome. Remote Viewing is very helpful in giving support to the defendant.

Interrogation

Interrogation is the act of getting to the 'truth' of the matter through consistent lines of questioning. We can interrogate ourselves, a partner, a friend, an employee or someone called the 'accused'. Interrogation can feel threatening to persons in everyday life, but can feel necessary in outing the truth if other areas of discussion are ineffective. Interrogation needs an access point into a person's open and honest state of awareness. To start off ask light questions that are easy to answer, make statements easy to relate to thus building up a rapport, giving the respect that you are 'under-standing' the person and respecting them. Then move to questions that are easy to answer in 'truth'. Once the person has started to communicate from this place of awareness and consciousness the interrogator holds them in the position of 'truth' consciousness by continuing down lines of questioning, digging deeper and deeper to look at what is under the issue, pushing at the whole truth, cross questioning and asking questions around the circumstance to find emotive - how they felt about things at that moment. Once a person shares emotional states of being they tend to then share their activity around their responses to those emotions, so it is possible to continue asking them ques- tions until the full understanding is reached. Intuition places a large role in finding direction with interrogation as it's so fast.

The person interrogates from a goal, 'the truth about where you were on....', 'or why you lied to me about ... ' Often people lie simply to protect themselves or the persons that could be hurt, so one way of outing is to bring awareness that protection was used in defence of the truth. The journey is in uncovering that information.

There needs to be a sense of non judgement when going through interrogation. The importance is in simply getting the truth and the whole picture, not in how to relate to it. It's a person-centered approach that leads someone to tell all.

Acknowledging all areas of lie, feelings, senses and questions around intuitive responses helps to move deeper into the journey of outing the truth. 'I sensed that there is more to what you are telling me'; 'Why do I get the feeling you are missing out information? What impact would the truth have on me? 'Don't undermine my ability to handle the truth'; 'I feel I deserve to know what really happened that day'; 'I feel you don't fully understanding how you are dis- empowering me by not being clear'; 'We all have to go through complicated circumstances'; 'Things sometimes get out of control'; 'Let me see if I can understand the whole picture'; 'I want to understand the truth'; 'Why were you motivated in this way?'; 'How do you find out this information?'; 'Sometimes we find things out that we shouldn't; sometimes we see things we don't want to see'; 'What happened that day that you felt was beyond your boundaries?'; 'Why are you hiding this knowledge?'; 'Let us see if I can understand.'

If they still cannot access the information, there is a way of helping them to re-live the circumstances by asking them to go on the journey back into their memories. Present day memories are stored in the head but hidden memories are often stored in the body.

Ask the person, 'Where in your body do you have a feeling associated with the story of what happened that day?' They point to a body part. Ask them to fully relax and take them into a meditation space, visualising going on a journey, as if taking a walk into that area of the body, allowing the minds eye to visualise the environment. They are on a pathway and can feel the ground under their feet, they notice the sensation of the weather, how they felt that day, the sensation of expectancy. Ask them to recall what they were wearing, then ask them to talk about the environment and how it looks to be there. Is there is anyone around? What are their characteristics? What are they wearing? If they are on their own and standing still, just allow them to be, let them take their time, wait with them, allowing the journey to unfold as fast or as slowly as their memories serve them to recall. In time they will recount this story and be able to answer all questions associated with it in truth.

The same process is used in past life regression, but a deeper state of meditation is invoked so that the soul can remember as far back as it needs to. Sometimes the memories arrive from the 'collective' rather than the individual, a story unfolds that is relevant to the persons healing. With collective stories there is no 'real' understanding of how reality is related to in truth, but the stories are very effective in bringing understanding and learning, and in changing circumstances for the person to move forward into a new reality.

Life between lives can also be accessed in a similar way but with an emphasis of going into the light and in soul identity. Going back even further, we can find planets of origin and enhance extra sensory perception of receptors used in different life forms. This is a creative space of awareness to enhance performance, consciousness, communication and identity. Sensitive soul travelers tend to embrace this experience, opening up to understanding historical information and multi-dimensional aspects in reality. Philosophical and scientific inspiration can be found by setting intentions in the same way an hypothesis is set in a journey of academic writing. Many plans and inspired activities in this space of creation can be understood and registered. This is the place of creation in collaboration with the universe, the universe knows all answers- it is up to us to ask the right questions.

Affirm - **I have the ability to be consciously active in empowering my life and communicating openly and honestly.**

Rewards

The right to receive rewards in life is achieved through a sense of personal value and understanding of the whole nature of the situation. Energies that bring the experience of reward need to be embraced with gratitude and allowance. Being open to receiving on all levels 'allows' the limitless possibility of having in. Learning to not judge the source of monies, or energies in receiving, enables a strong potential of pathway into having. I have a donation button on my website that is simply there in case anyone feels like giving. This potential enables extra gifting without formal agreement, it is often used. I am always grateful to those who give.

Looking at what you are receiving from others can help assess ways of moving forward, in ways that reward beyond financial benefit. Other ways of receiving are through compassion, healing, gifting, companionship, intimacy, security, inspiration, connection to the experience or journey, creative expression, respite, peace, love, humour, adventure, communion or union.

If a person is receiving and they want to share the experience, relationship or project with another, the benefits they have may not be able to be shared with the third party. This can isolate a person from joy, and can isolate the benefits of the experience to the individuals in which the experience was created.

There also can be rewards from a relationship that satisfy one person's interests but not others in a group or family. This means the relationships have to be managed accordingly. Realising the benefits you gain from your situation, project or development phase and looking at how others relate to it, can help you to understand if they can share in any rewards.

What are the rewards and benefits of working with this project or person? Relating to this person? Walking down this path?

Are these rewards able to be shared? By whom can they be shared? How can I expand on these relationships or experiences?

When we invest in a person over time, we may initially invest unconditionally. However over time, if we find ourselves not having much more energy to give, it may be that we are not feeling inspired enough or that we are noticing we aren't receiving much reward through those investments. We may have noticed that the person is drawing us in and we are not feeling inspired to give further. There is therefore a need to analyse how the persons around us can be rewarded for our choices and share in our benefits of work, home and family. The expectation that something of a 'reward' will come back in quality of time, inspiration, shared joy or financial benefit, may not actually expand into the world of other people's lives or reality. There can then be a feeling of wanting or needing 'something back'. The person can feel, 'everyone wants bits of me'. They may not realise how much energy of others they are feeding off to enable their activities to be sustainable. An introvert tends to energetically feed off their own internal world: an extro-vert feeds and nourishes themselves off others and surrounds themselves with people to feed. A balance can work, but often an introvert understands the feeling of 'taking energy' and will only take from those inspired to give. An introvert will often back away from a relationship if he or she feels that too much energy is being claimed. This can create confusion as the energy was originally unconditional. However the introvert's world is very delicate and the sense of harmony has to be nurtured and nourished on a detailed level, which means a sense of detachment has to be created whilst the dynamics are re-addressed.

If you are unsure whether or not to be involved with someone, ask, 'How does this person add value to my life?' The answer may be specific and focussed or it may be expansive and limitless. Having an understanding enables an intuitive response to managing those relationships. The same question could be asked to the other person, 'How do I, or can I help you?'. Their answer may be again focused and specific or it may be expansive and limitless. If one of the persons is specific, that is the likely outcome as unless they are inspired to give in other areas, they will cause the relationship to be limited by their own vision. You can always go on to ask, 'Out of all the other areas I am inspired to create with you, which ones do you see happening? Which ones would you like to see through?' Often one person holds dreams, visions and ideas that the other hasn't thought of. Their role may be to bring ideas and vision to manifestation if they have a collaborative and willing partner. If those dreams, visions and ideas are projected without agreement, the person will feel used. Their energy will drain and there will be a time of detachment. By knowing who consents to invest energy in dreams, visions and ideas, with an understanding of benefits, helps to remain focused on constructive pathways of understanding. There is a dependability in those who share the same vision as they are inspired to create and work at the same goal. They are the ones who will see the project through. If you are sure of the vision, or dream, or project you really want to create, but are unsure if the people around you are in agreement, ask, 'Does this being serve the greater vision?'; 'Does this being feel inspired to give to the project'. You are really asking if the people around you have the energy to commit to the project. This information is useful, as if the answer is only a few weeks or months, you know where you are at and can keep on asking others to combine their interests and inspired ideas with your vision.

Most projects are then dealt with sensitively through this conscious way of communication. The project manager, producer or director may not be fully aware of the values with which they are operating, or the inspiration or benefits others are feeding off. However there are simple ways of exposing these components. Understanding the values you want to work with helps to create a community and culture that others can grow with. Expressing them in everyday communication, helps to advertise a culture and community that knows its ethics and codes and conducts. This enables a peaceful environment that nurtures communion - a reward in itself.

Often the contract process in conscious understanding, shares the values intending to work by. These then can be called upon when any part of the project seems out of alignment. Conscious people tend to be honourable and dependable, but there is a need to encourage finances to cover all development phases. Due to passions, sometimes some areas of funding can be overlooked. It is important to value the details and understand rewards and benefits in a shared process of integration.

Intuitive Conflict Resolution

Intuitive conflict resolution is reached through the active listening and understanding of persons:

- Highest Priority Intentions/Goals

- Values

- Understanding or respect of the person's role

- Understanding of vision or goals and differences in visions or goals

- Understanding of different persons 'realities' or experiences of problem

- Boundaries

- True Nature

- Expectations

- Emotive

- Needs

- Pathways and Underlying Agendas

- Options

- Delivery

- Pathways forward

All of these areas of understanding can be reached by asking the correct questions to parties concerned. Or, through collective consciousness, one person can use their intuition to 'read' into the energies of all persons involved, enabling a deeper understanding of limits, interferences, underlying agendas, emotive, corruption, insecurities, boundaries, pathways, outcomes and directive approaches. This deeper approach is often more effective as the arrival into understanding tends to be in wisdom, empathy, in truth and with a peaceful aim.

The individual, when actively listening in to their inner truth, by using the 'Sacred River of Truth Meditation', will be able to attune to hearing their inner wisdom and understanding of the bigger picture, around all conflict. Finding areas of shared 'value' often brings the area of conflict into an area of growth, enabling learning as a priority outcome. With a new pathway of development, the situation moves forward. This brings priority to newly learnt values and the development process of integrating them to new practice. New areas of practice encourage a strong secure framework of foundation that enables change and development with adjustments and respect to needs, wants and pathways. Fully understanding the values, by looking at their definition and history, adds a huge skill-set of value to experience. Are you experienced?

Yes I am. I know the values we need to operate from to deliver on this project are.....

Yes I am. I know the values I need to work with to encourage this relationship to flourish are....

Yes I am. I know that the values we need to help us creatively integrate are...

Yes I am. I know that the values we need to work with to enable our marriage to work are...

Yes I am. I know that the values we need to work with, to be able to collaborate the values are...

Values that are helpful to create peace in conflict :

Unity, equality, non judgement, reward, understanding of ..., connection to resources, integrity, honour, openness, empathy, unconditional love, allowance, active investment (time, energy, money, quality of experience etc.), reward, acceptance, active connection, understanding to emotive, safety in vulnerability, non-violent communication, opportunity for change, growth, active listening, the enabling of expansion.

Question - What other values do I like to work with? What other areas of my life could be expanded on with value adding to experience?

By affirming powerful values that are agreeable to all parties, we tend to higher the quality of the experience and performance into delivery. We create a new sense of contract in which high values are adhered to.

Change Management

Moving people from one position to another, often brings up conflicts and disagreement. The previous list helps to troubleshoot some of those worries, however in programs of change, we often have to prepare people's expectations, give voice, reassurance, security and a sense of value. The type of investment energy in persons who need to go on a journey of change is very important to ensuring a healthy delivery. Temporary working communities can be nurtured through environments that enable nomadic culture, encouraging a flexibility and adaptability. Developing people into their inner sense of security is very important, as they may have performed for the company and added to the experience they have in their role, to give them a sense of security. This sense of security suddenly appears artificial. There is a need for an approach to re-assure and encourage the adventure of change with a circumstance of uprooted expectation, enabling a security through a healthy arrival at a new destination or project with clarity, active listening, active understanding and reward. Often with a lot of change all security is stripped away from the individual. This loss of trust and dependability in those who initiated the re-structure or change in circumstances has to be dealt with through active listening, dependability, financial reassurance, risk assessment, inspired outcome, unity, vision, intuitive understanding, self-value, love, development and stress release. The feeling of unity can encourage a deep peace and be an enabler. Bringing awareness to the 'controls', how the environment can work for the people involved can help them to reassess opportunity and potential in working with the situation allowing a consciously transforming journey in which all persons are working towards a common objective.

However if an area of competition is introduced, the ability to feel union without security can cause corruption and political dynamics. Timing and sensitive resolution with a more casual approach of team work 'feedback', constructive development conversations, opening up, rather than formal processes, can encourage change to be adaptable and flexible without the pressures of a killing ground of redundancies etc. Formal processes can be arranged at final stages and with a person-centered career development aim. Giving reassurance of support in the personal development of the individual adds value to the sensory perception of experience, helping them arrive at a new destination with or without the company, using their gained rewards to positive effect.

Constructive Development into Person-Centered Security; Internal Communications to Create a New Culture and Environment

What are my strengths?

What are my 'unique' added values and attributes?(I am open, articulate, approachable, humorous, well presented, intuitive, logical, I use common sense etc..)

What are my dreams?

What are my needs?

What lifestyle would I like to live?

What would need to happen to achieve this goal?

If I could have anything in my life what would it be?

What do I see as the biggest hurdle in my life?

What do I need in my life to move through this hurdle?

What would I like to achieve during this journey?

How can I feel better about myself?

How much do I feel a sense of belonging or fitting in? How deep is that?

How isolated do I feel?

How do I feel about my work colleagues? How can this improve?

What values would I like in my work relationships?

Can I initiate a sense of spirited fun/achievement/passion to the people around me?

Which values are important to me in team spirit or working relationships?

Do I feel inspired? How can I connect more to inspired thinking?

Do I feel actively heard?

Who 'sees' me and believes in me?

How far- reaching is my impact on this environment?

What else is possible?

What are my options?

What do I need to do to actively explore these pathways?

The process of looking at primary values in working relationships and working process has the potential to enable a sense of healthy experience whilst going through change. Unifying values that are shared, combined with a sense of communication encourages communion. Aligning relationships with an understanding of common goals, high values, the nature of team spirit within the culture of the environment encourages change from within the individual that is person centered and comes from an inspired place of opportunity. Enabling all persons to feel they are growing, expanding and their needs are being heard. Giving person centered emotional security to the individual in their personal journey in understanding their needs even if their future direction is highlighted to be different enables a housing for change and new direction. The personal sense of liberation and lightness experienced through strong emotional support, enables an uprooted experience in which the entity, organisation or company sets off, like a ship lifting up it's anchor. This abstract state of movement enables restructuring, strategy and new direction to form, giving the right environment for growth, change and expansion.

Orgasm5 - Relating to the Greek orgasmos, excitement, swelling, also sexual climax.

10 SACRED RELATIONSHIP

The profound bliss we experience when in union with a deeply connected soulmate may be one of the hardest factors to put into words. Over the years, being able to digest the elements that invite a state of pure love in heavenly uplift has possibly been a journey of maturity. One has to abandon one's thoughts to fully engage in the understanding of the experience.

There are elements that I have recognised in this union, which enable me to be able to express the nature of sexuality for a 'sensitive' person. I started to refer to this as almost a different sexual orientation. The components are:

'Sensual Sexuality'

- The union relates through attuned touch, clairvoyance, divine channelling, loving words, downloading from source, when the energies are engaged with and built up. The union is often supported by and nurtured by God, divine beings and angels.

- The union of the two souls is ageless and not related to through visual aspects but sensory perception and experience.

- The journey unfolds through deep memories in the soul, shifting through centuries of experience and understanding, with connections to physical environments, locations and memories in those environments.

- The soulmate meets you in everything you are not, you meet them in everything you are and they are not; in gender, intelligence, security, creativity and skill set.

- The union brings a close relationship to oneness and connects on all levels of experience, in the physical, emotional, energetic and spiritual body.

- The union of sex or lovemaking enables the beloveds to share their energies in information technology, blueprint, initiation and bonding, building up the sexual energy, containing the energies within the two; an expansive vessel of peaceful, loving, pure, erotic, light energy.

- The depth of love means that tolerance is like a timeless patience, anger is lost, anger is replaced by questions in the presence of love.

- The love is fully unconditional and is expressed without judgement.

- The journey unfolds, often illogically, seemingly with hurdles but due to the timeless nature of experience, the pathway finds its own direction; you know you want the best for each other and will love beyond selfish need.

- You feel held in love, in a secure and nurturing space that appears to give architecture to the days and minutes.

- There is an ability to allow your partner to be in their truth, transparent and free, aspiring to a benevolent outcome to all persons involved in the union.

- The energies between you guide, empower and give deliverance to the love of God. You operate from the divine will of the Creator.

Beyond Sexuality

We know when we first meet a friend, colleague or partner whom we connect with, our energies raise into an excited life-giving sense of euphoria. We feel at ease knowing we are free to carry out our life journey and speak our truth in how we digest our experiences, disappointments, vulnerabilities and joys. We know we have shared interest in our journey and we are able to connect in the ways we are met, with reward and experience. We find the energy is constructive and dependable; our hearts open and we feel the tug on our muscles as the energy pours out in love and adoration of the person we have met. Over time, we may find that this feeling of open-hearted experience gets squashed or reduced; there may be a sense of limit or resistance in being fully open in an open heart of experience. This resistance is often a sense of uncertainty or doubt - a worry about self-sacrificing elements that may present in the process of relationship.

Nurturing a healthy heart space for relationship is about releasing insecurities, jealousy, fears, disappointments and pains, by acknowledging them and giving the energies back to where they came from.

We may also be resistant to fully trusting the union of whole-hearted relationship. Half-hearted situations present as lovers, muse, mistress or companion. They are relationships in which only a fraction of experience is allowed in. The resistance is normally caused by unresolved foundations, a defensive heart around responsibility and trust to the surrendering to the journey of experience. To be able to move forward it is important to seek a whole heart as an individual and to claim the right of honouring your heart space with a love that flows from a limitless source, exploring the limitless potential in experience through the deep embodying of a relationship based on true love. However there may be reasons why you do not trust in the love of your heart or the flow. In the process of allowing love in, it is important to clear any interference or sense of locking out or casting out. This may be for countless personal reasons, often relating to past memories of pain, rejection or abandonment. We may also have found a true love in a soul mate but they may be with another, as a lot of relationships come to people through circumstance or children. The process of unravelling truth and developing an honest understanding of your situation, you can see what kind of relationship story is unravelling and start clearing the resistance, we may have created coping strategies to protect from rejection but these defence systems may not fully serve a fully open heart. Early experiences of rejection or emotional neglect from parents are relevant to the reasons we choose lovers, sometimes we fall for someone that counterbalances our deepest pain. To clear, we can do a meditation that serves over time. Once the resistance is cleared, it is possible to claim back the heart space and manage a pathway to true love. What are the limitless possibilities of experience in entering into a light and blissful state of understanding, relationship and creativity?

'The blessings of full-hearted love need honour and courage in the path of surrendering that no longer relates to the shadows of self and others but the trust in union and light of the love of a dependable universe, God'.

Meditation to Clear Resistance - Blissing out the Heart

Whilst sitting comfortably, I invite you to turn your thoughts to your breath, emptying your mind of all concerns or worries. Focus on the air you breathe into your lungs as it goes on to oxygenate the cells in your blood stream. Imagine the breath to be like a clear light that is loving and pure and able to illuminate and invoke your soul into its deepest memories and open state of awareness. With every breath, allow a deep letting go on the out breath, releasing thoughts, feelings and a sense of physicality, slowly dropping down into a deep and relaxed state. With every breath, concentrate on expanding on the light and love of the air you breathe and the journey it makes in illuminating the soul, letting your body fully relax as you sink into a deep state of peace. Allow an expansion of light energy to work through your chakras and bring a sense of deep peace as the light brightens and purifies, as the energies extend beyond the physical to connect with the lightness all around. As you allow your breathing to relax you, please focus on your heart and a sense of arrival, remembering what it is to be open- hearted, maybe remembering a meeting with someone whom you loved dearly or when you experienced orgasm and your heart poured out with a sense of divine light. As you provoke these memories, allow yourself to drop through your heart and bathe in the energies of bliss and euphoria, enjoying a baptism of deep love and warmth, breathing deeply into the bliss, bathing in the sense of depth in the Holy Spirit and the infinity of creation.

Then take a moment to go to the heart, the circular sense of open heart and notice if the heart is open, closed or held in a place of limit and if there are any shadows or persons around the heart.

Please meditate on the vision, seeing what can be done to clear the energy around the heart, asking those who are taking heart space without responsibility, to leave. Ask those who limit to take a step back or leave and those who constantly undermine, to leave. Look for any sense of heaviness and spend time breathing into it, clearing it. Look for any sense of resistance in fully embracing the love and light in. Affirming, I allow love and light to flow through me, I allow my heart to be open. I allow the divine to flow through me. I am love, I am peace, I am the infinite flow of heart. There may be visions that present that represent your resistance to light and love flowing through you. Just mediate on them allowing them to change, gently massaging the heart area if struggling to get movement, or breathing deeply through the images until experiencing a flow of source energy that uplifts and elevates to a state of euphoric bliss, repeating, I am the infinite flow of heart. As the energy ascends you will find you dissolve the physical surroundings, breaking into a new space of illumination of pure white diamond light energy, connecting you with the heart of God, and multiplying in its blessings of uplifted peace.

Coupling

When making love with the 'beloved', a couple relating on a soul level, will experience a 'latching on' to each other both on an open heart level and sexual level. The women especially notices this experience whilst making love and after. She will connect to the 'other' beyond lovemaking through a natural sense of commitment. The natural instinct at the beginning for the man is to detach and disconnect post love making, the strength of the emotional bond evolved in the start up period allows a holding space in which the latching on of the heart finds a consistent place of love and intimacy. A man will find this process easier to accept by 'holding the women' and focusing on her energy, so that there is less sabotage in the relationship(man's instinct to 'kill' off the relationship only serves on a primal level). Once the process of integration and bonding is accepted, we take the courage to work through and communicate resistance; a sense of closing down, fear of attachment, fear of commitment, underlying coping strategies. These aspects can be expressed and allowed to air. Eventually we are able to find the voice of our heart, allowing the soft words of unconditional love to find a temple or sacred space of understanding, engagement and loyalty. The honour found here allows the relationship to grow, develop and sustain a healthy and entrusted journey of love making and sacred relationship, the relationship is nurtured and nourished through the sweet voice of the abundant and graceful loving heart.

Remote Viewing

Remote Viewing through clairvoyant vision is a very powerful way of listening to the truth in others, relationships and in projects. I use this sacred tool a lot. We can use remote viewing to look beyond our relationship hurdles or insecurities, tuning in to the true nature of the situation.

Viewing a person or situation in its truth, when they are not present or you don't have all the information around the circumstance, gives collective consciousness the opportunity to guide you, by asking questions relevant to the nature of experience.

This can be done by visualising a person, by tuning in to their name or character and 'reading' the energy around them as you visualise an image of them.

For privacy reasons I only tune in if I feel it's appropriate from a place of benevolence. For projects, I use the name of the project. All information around the nature of the circumstance, their struggles, limits, needs can be gained in respect through remote viewing. I am sure this skill was how we coped with separation before telephones.

To try remote viewing yourself, please go in to a meditative state, imagine the person you want to understand or get to know near a river or in front of you, look as if you mean to get down to the truth of the situation. I use my hands a lot to tune in around these aspects. My hands are very attuned to the energies around, but others use clairvoyance, clairsentience or clairaudience. It is very important not to project. Ask the question, 'what is the true nature of (persons) situation?' and wait for the information to come, delve deeper by developing your questions, allowing the universe to meet you with a response. The development of this skill leads to a high level of skill set in the natural technology of being human.

When you have big questions in relationship or questions about commitment or honesty, remote viewing is very helpful to get to the bottom of what is happening. I can see if a person is entwined with another, the kind of relationship they are in with that person, if they are insecure, if they are feeling limited. I also can see what is needed to help them and to move the situation forward. All movements are catalysed with energy, spiritual energy/Reiki and love, even the most complex set of circumstances. The power of loving the person in this way can bring profound outcomes and deeper union and understanding. By giving the person in the vision energy, we often see their circumstance unravel and their healing. This often changes the nature of the relationship and brings trust or openness.

When doing the same on a project, I find it possible to look at strategy, direction, investment money, the team, partnerships, the development phases, strategies with communication, markets, time lines and project phases. These are very valuable areas to work with.

Beyond Bliss

With every high, there seems to be a low, which means living on the level of orgasmic bliss day to day is hard to sustain. So we have to understand the combination of passion, love and mission in creating a union in the energies enabling soul mate, direction, mission and love to come together. The nurture of these energies comes to us from love - from a place of kindness, understanding, dependability and friendship. This is the central system of operation as it keeps us on a plateau of limitless possibility. Passion and compassion encourage a divine surrender into the abyss of magical euphoria, in which the expansive wise universe shows itself in pure illumination. This restores and nourishes us but can cause us a certain level of personal sacrifice. Orgasms help us to stay in a place of positive experience in which we can manifest from the seat of our power. Men need orgasm for a different reason to women. Men need orgasm for release of self-expression and to take them away from their head, egos and release from desire, which is ironic in the sense they may objectify to then experience bonding through sensory intimacy. For women, enjoying the orgasm as a regular and intimate experience is important in connecting with love, the higher conscious, the divine, care and sensory experience. Sustaining a regular and nourishing relationship with bliss is very important for all of us, in nurture, feeling strong and emotional connection.

When developing on an energetically tantric level, the energies and frequencies instruct and inspire the activities, giving the freedom of unconditional love, transparency, security and a wealth of understanding associated to experience and the energies of divine creation, enabling our sense of bliss energy to reach heights beyond words. These journeys of love-making encourage a surrendering to the will of the divine. This ultimate sacrifice of giving ourselves on so many levels, leads us on a journey into deliverance, to the surrender of trust in God and union but we can only centre on that journey from a place of love, understanding and kindness. We can see that the passions and desires of personal will can destroy us, if we sacrifice ourselves in a way that sometimes leaves us with a need for restoration and relief or respite. We therefore have to balance our experiences and the gentleness of our lives to the understanding of the nourishment and nurture of our energies, through love, the love of ourselves, our loved ones, the love of work, of persons and of life, keeping the experiences in harmony and balance with other parts or activities in our lives.

Understanding the role of 'Divine Mother and Father' allows a gentle love to inform. When we have realised the central point of balance is love, we are in a place of creativity, of development and growth, in which the universe serves us as much as we serve it. Keeping in touch with our eroticism helps us to keep connected to our seat of power, but we need our hearts to connect through our pelvis and to be aligned to our connections in both our heart and sexuality. We find a place of divine birthright in the delicate harmony of living, realising that through love, understanding, dependability and kindness we are in a constant, expanding and developing pathway of growth. Our life can therefore be content and elevated in a way that satisfies us and our sensory experience of living. Through understanding how the energies inspire, how we are directed into growth, we reach a plane of understanding that is consistent and expansive. Holding nurturing space for male and female energies to develop, grow and regenerate as they express themselves in all areas of consciousness, we hold, we listen and accept each other wholly so that we have the space to become.

Consuming Life through the Heart

Through the following of our hearts, we make conscious decisions about our work, relationships and what we consume: materially, spiritually, emotionally and in being able to open our hearts and take others in. Historically, the act of moving away from the ego into the heart, then re-asserting the sexual act of consuming others as a collective, meant persons engaged with open relation- ships, group sexual acts such as orgies, collective intima- cy, or magick. This ability to take in another without ANY judgement, in tolerance and with understanding is an admirable level of enlightenment but not for everyone. The journey back to oneness and bliss is definitely rele- vant to orgasm and sexual engagement, taking into account that our sexuality is a foundation to our power, our light and our love.

However as I have explained the journey is not always to become one, as a collective. There are very honourable reasons why the ingestion of others on a heart level is not necessary at different stages of the journey. Protecting ourselves from emotional toxicity, from ego or from being taken advantage of, is a form of self- love. We are not simply vessels for the darker more aggressive forms of creation to flow through: war, murder, organised crime, anger, rape etc. We are not here to simply facilitate the whole of creation to flow through us; we are here to honour ourselves and others with self- love.

The act of allowing creation to flow through is an act of opening up to the source of creation, an act to be done from a place of 'Source'; the matrix of the universe in light. This means anchoring with lightness and creating our world from a place of love and light and enabling our relationships and our work to be creative in lifestyle from a place of beauty, development, growth and prosperity. Therefore, we need to assess if someone is genuinely communicating and creating their world from a loving place, a light place or another source of chaos. We start to operate in the light of creation.

Awareness of the foundations of eternal soul relation-ships, through past life memory, helps us to understand the karmic nature of the relationship. Some relationships can be healed just through levels of forgiveness, under-standing, shared learning. Others can be understood, forgiveness can be given then new pathways can be sought. We don't have to stay in a relationship that doesn't work.

We can see our soul 'commitments' in trust and work with the relationships in love, to enable an unfolding.

Sometimes our destiny chooses to support the development of slightly limited experiences. Other times these avenues are resolved through other experiences of intimacy, which is why polyamorous relationships can work when there is a fully acknowledged understanding of the depth of experience encountered. When the needs of persons we are relating to are satisfied beyond the primary relationship we can choose to understand and support the development. The choice of commitment, exposure and honour in these complexities can enable a trusted outcome. A love triangle is a strong structure, within polyamorous activity, often built on a foundation of trust. However, finding more individually expansive relationships with less limits can encourage a more resourceful experience of living, in which all needs are satisfied by the depth and intensity of experience. When we relate on a soul level and have the infinite experiences of 3,000 earth years, 4,000 space years and inter planetary activity all available to us, we rarely need to look beyond the other. We mirror each other as the universe: we are the wild adventurers, the starlight, the unfolding passion, the soul traveller, we all and all is one.

Being able to trust that those around us have benevolence in mind, gives confidence in the way we relate and build security. The security is a form of dependability that enables our faith in the universe and in the collective to deliver us to a continued state of growth, development, energy, happiness and love.

Activating Bliss

The bliss energy is understood as experienced in the energetic expansion of orgasm. This energy can be nurtured
and nourished on a daily basis through meditation and
breath work. The sexual energy we hold in the base our
spine, our root chakra can be held within us and expanded
upon through nourishment and nurture within our whole
body; allowing us to stay uplifted and with the experience
of the sexual energies on a daily level. This enables us to
stay seated in the roots of our power without needing a
relationship or to attach to intimacy unless it genuinely
serves us.

By holding the energy within, we allow ourselves to
concentrate on loving acts in intimacy in communion,
allowing ourselves to love each other in gentle and sensitive ways, freeing us to become more self centered in
holding power with our sexuality. Sharing our sacred
sexual attributes with a special person or honouring our
space with divine understanding in the mirror of God can
be encouraged through a collective understanding of
oneness.

Seeding our heart space and sexual experience in sensual
ways with agreements of care, love, understanding, needs
and dependability allows us to develop deep and connected relationships with people in our life, allowing the intimacy of loving touch and companionship to fulfill and

satisfy us without unhealthy needs, or wanting more than we have. We always have every thing we need each day.

Meditation for the Individual or Partners

To enable sexual energy to integrate and hold power we can activate our sexual energy by focusing on the energy in our root chakra and how it relates to our physical body, we can also make a direct link through visualisation with our pineal gland. To activate our pineal gland we can put one of our hands behind our neck, the other on our fore-head. This position releases stress, it is a holding position. We can then visualise our minds eye in our pineal gland and visualise drawing a white cord of light down to our root chakra and the muscles around the root chakra of the anus, the sexual muscles and the urinary muscles.

We can get to know the areas of muscle by contracting and releasing. So we can start by taking a deep breath down through the pineal in to the root chakra and holding the breath for a few seconds whilst contracting the anus. We then release the breath and let go of all thoughts and feelings, releasing any tension. We can then take another breath, pulling the energy of light down from the pineal into the root chakra and contracting the anus again, holding the breath for a few seconds, then releasing.

We then move to the sexual muscles around the vagina and the penis (the corpus cavernosum). The penis is not a muscle and relies on the vagina as a muscle in union, so the muscles used to activate the sexual energy in the individual male are the perineum(in between the anus and the scrotum or vagina) and the sphincter (urethra muscle).

We will concentrate on the perineum in this moment. By breathing again from the pineal gland down the column of the self, through to the root chakra, here we contract the perineum, holding the muscles for a few seconds, then releasing and allowing and expansion of energy to move. We allow our sexual muscles to fully relax by releasing.

We then start again, drawing breath in from the nose, to the lungs, up to the pineal gland then down to the root chakra, holding the perineum and holding the breath for a few seconds, then releasing the muscles allowing the energies to expand.

Women can now include the contraction of the vagina whilst contracting the perineum, holding the breath for a few seconds and then releasing, men carry on focusing on the perineum.

As the energy builds we can develop the breath work, breathing out through the mouth and taking breath in through the nose, visualising oxygen as white light. Allowing a circular breath in and out. By now we can release the hands from behind the neck and forehead. Allowing ourselves to become more submerged in the breathing and the contraction and release of the muscles, noticing how the energy builds and the sensory aspects magnify.

We finally take our attention to the sphincter, at the front of the pelvis, noting the contraction of this muscle and the sensation on our bladder, taking a deep breath through our nose, running light down from the pineal gland to the root chakra contracting the muscles in out sphincter, holding the breath and releasing the out breath through our mouth.

We then take breath in through our nose, to our pineal drawing the energy down the central column into our root chakra and contract all the muscles in our root chakra, allowing the energies to really build and expand. Holding the breath as the energy moves through our whole body and sensory perception.

To hold this energy we then move to motion of circular breathing in which we take deep breaths in through our nose and release on the out breath. Allowing any shifts or changes, any emotions to be present and release, by gently acknowledging our selves and our feelings every step of the way. We may start channelling energies or visions as the experience expands. Allow the journey to inspire.

We can also share the energy with a partner, doing the exercise together. We do this by using our intuition to guide us, exploring the channelled energy that communicates through the energy body, with sensual and erotic movements from our physical body and catalysts through contact with our partner.

Partners

If with a partner, we encourage all senses to open and attune, through sensual activity. Opening up the vagina by gentle circular massages deep inside and around the walls, preparing the penis with long strokes, beyond the shaft and including the anus. When ready the female needs time to connect to the penis, to ingest the wholeness of the shaft with her vagina and to share an attuned sexual experience. This direct sense of connection, in holding the penis with her internal muscles leads to a feeling of oneness and allows the heart to open. Giving this experience time, through open senses and feelings allows the energy body or soul presence to 'latch on' to each other.

Finding attunement and connection, allows an expansion in to the universal energies, tuning in, will give guidance to you in to different positions, movements, to bring alignment to the physical experience, to encourage different spaces of intimacy and connection, energising your sensuality, each other, allowing the energy to channel through and be shared. Feel how it becomes enhanced, giving a sense of dance or energetic exchange to sexual expression, allow the energetic experience to build up in to a euphoric state.

We can allow intuition to guide us in a build up as approaching orgasm, by keeping all senses open and bringing awareness to the open heart. The heart chakra opens automatically, this is an honour to share as it opens a channel of unconditional love. We can share this moment with grace and gratitude, allowing the energies to catalyse an embodiment with the divine, a boundless love that fills us as vessels of creation. This may catalyse our intuition or clairvoyance, leading us in to a visual journey or channelled experience, opening up our spirituality and connection with the divine. Allowing ourselves fulfilment through the heart chakra by breathing the energies though deeply whilst holding a sense of deep engagement, eventually gives an uplift from our heart into our higher conscious, expressing a warm, light and nourishing orgasm that allows a deep connection with the care and attention of a loving universe. Hold presence and space in the experience.

Coming Down

In time we allow our breathing to return to normal and to enjoy the physical embodiment of our sexual energy with our heart energy, enabling us to stay seated in our power and in the bliss energy of creation as the energies have expanded us into our omnipresence as a universal being.

Notice how the energy in the root chakra and the self, becomes clear, centered and strong, giving you grace and uplift as you move in to the grounded state of physical awareness.

Continuing to hold each other enables a space to form in which clarity and clearing created by 'Source' can communicate. The divine presence, allows a strong space of 'peace' in which it is possible to share vulnerabilities with another, naturally communicate emotional aspects. Holding each other during this time frame is constructive to relationship, communication and the sharing of vulnerabilities, giving a high quality experience in emotional intimacy.

Beyond the union of divine energies, invite Mother Earth to embody you and hold you, lay nestled in trust. If an active day follows, plant your feet firmly on the ground and as you move through the rest of the day, this gives grounding and protects the energies you have shared or downloaded.

Resistance

Sometimes it is hard to trust in another's resistance; they simply are not ready to act from a position of lightness and may push away and withdraw. Resistance causes an erosion of trust (dependability and understanding), resistant is the inability to surrender to love and light and

follow pathways that enable happiness. We must unconditionally love ourselves, our body, our mind and our soul
to be able to tolerate and accept the other. This takes a
deep commitment and loyalty to our true sense of self.

This can be painful as consuming another on a heart level
is an act of being in love, you may want to bridge, or
reach out. However the most useful way of dealing with
resistance is to let it be and let transformation and understanding come in time. If one party implements controls
to the situation, it is hard to move on or detach, it is therefore important to discuss the nature of the impact of their
actions from an emotional perspective, explaining how
they make you feel. However, once this is done and the
energies are free, it is possible to detach and inspire yourself in light, affirming the strength of living and creating
from a place of light and love. Meeting others already
sure they want to create their world from a place of love,
kindness and development of self, means that the relationships should sustain without too much resistance,
however we all have deeper protections or coping strategies which have to be shared and moved through as we
go on the journey to deeper relationship. Trusting in the
nature of deeply connected hearts allows a synergy and
profound sense of experience in which the soul benefits
from a deep satisfaction that is intimate and life giving.

Karma

I look at karma from a point of soul adjustment, taking in to consideration all past lives and future outcomes. I arrange meetings with the Karmic board, in the library of soul books, many call the akashi records. By going to this library in a visualisation, taking the book that is about your soul life and then visualising walking to the back of the library to meet with the board of karma. I invite you to look at the nature of the book, how light the contents feel and to scan the pages around life stories, dramas, history. At the back of the library around a table, simiar to a conference table, we find elders that can help us understand our life paths, lessons and soul adjustments. We can undersand why our life may differ to the normal expectations and what lessons we are learning. Lessons are simply 'values', like learning to be compassionate, joyful, expansive, limtless, loving, dependable, understanding, vulnerable, wise. Many find their trauma hard to resolve or understand from a karmic postion, this library and consultation with the elders gives the ability to find some peace, understanding and awareness. Often we can go into a past life regression through scanning the book. There are also screens, in which scenes of soul history and soul stories can be played back to the person, so they can see the complexity of their karma. The feeling of soul history and karma being seen as a story helps the impact of trauma to become lighter and more integrated as a historical experience taking time to find balance and harmony.

What is the nature of your Soul Book? What lessons are you learning in this lifetime?

Soul Identity

Understanding our design from origin helps to assess our purpose in this life, we often become limited from various past lives, through history and hundreds of years of challenge and growth. Reconnecting to our identity at source helps us to re-centre and let go of overlay identities and ways of relating to the world that take us away from our authenticity. I invite people to go to bardo, life between lives, and look at the environment they dwell in inbetween lives, to help them see their primary motivations and needs in being and functioning in their primary identity. I call this energetic environment a studio (of practice). For instance when I first did this meditation myself I found that in my studio I had a number of human size energy crystals that were shaped slightly differently, my job was to reset spiritual beings energy at source, by inviting their souls to recentre themselves by placing them in the centre of the crystal. As if re-programming the person back to their harmonious state without any projections, falsehoods, insecurities or pain. By reading A Life of Bliss we can see the connection, which isn't direct but a foundation of service. I help people back in to their true nature of being, security and experience in the world. Another spiritual being may find they help people pass through death or grow soul children: the children that die as babies. There are messengers, catalysts, light workers and nurturers. Many have sacrificed much in early child hood expereinces or mid life, to be able to serve more wholesomely and consistantly, through learning the importance of living with certain 'understandings' in nurturing healing life. What are the main values are you learning and expressing in this life time?

323

Harmony

When we have realised the central point of balanced living and service is love, we are in a place of creativity, of development and growth, in which the universe serves us, as much as we serve it.

By knowing the order or 'logos' of our life experience we create a safe space internally in which we can surrender to ourselves. We are free as we know how to relate, find our presence, intimacy, success and revel in achievement. We start to make our life in to an orgy of limitless possibilities, knowing how to honour and respect the heart, in service, well being and joy. We start to enter in to a blissful state of experience, that enables the everyday to be magical and the journey of surrendering into ourselves to lead us in a direction that serves us in universal understanding, love and union.

The phenomenon we become is a journey of truth that relates to our origin, we see our reflection as a mirror of creation. An sublime understanding and consciousness, as if looking from the eyes of God. We realise we are connected to everything and we embody all that is amongst creation as a playground of possibilities that we can love and nourish in to growth, creating the best possible outcome. We find the keys of universal understanding, love and bliss.

Oneness- The abridging of time, presence, union, mindful-
ness, purpose, grace, God, collective consciousness and
love. The quality or state of being one, singleness in
wholeness; a condition of perfect harmony or accord.

11 Oneness

Oneness is found through the surrender of freewill so as to allow a deep connection with others and with the heart of the conscious universe, God. This sacred surrender is made through a deep trust in the dependability of ourselves, all things and of our journey with others. When we fully nurture this state of being, we let others, whom may be resistant to understanding the bigger picture, a freedom. We have to let go, otherwise we get caught up in their resistance and this stops us from surrendering in bliss. Those who are resistant to collaborating with you, the collective consciousness or God will find a place that suits them and their quest. The freedom given to all is an allowance and an acceptance; an allowance to be where you need to be. By letting go of bridges, of wanting change or to be compassionate but by simply being, we allow presence in, love in and we give ourselves the free-dom to keep walking into the light, through a growth and nurture of blissful living in love.

Union or agreement allows unity to become ONE in peace, with those who truly understand the mysteries of the universe and their calling. To nurture and nourish a personal deep love and bliss that can be sustained can be done by taking care of one's self and enabling wisdom, freedom, lightness in living, so as to tread lightly and supportively through life's hurdles, allowing the support of the collective and of God to enable success and reward.

We are now in a position to create our reality from a posi-tion of lightness, in understanding, love, kindness, humour and bliss. The most important factors are uncon-ditional love, non judgement and tolerance. Love enables allowance and acceptance of the self and others. We can then extend into the allowance of the other in honour. Honour is the space of celebration in each other, in an acknowledgement of the value we share in each other's lives. When we fully appreciate and are grateful for the relationships, we are in a position of lightness and bliss as we can fully surrender to the trust of those relationships without resistance.

Non Duality

Letting go of duality means letting go of shadow aspects of the soul, of finding simplicity in peace, light and source, allowing yourself to be empowered by your own source. By unpinning or detaching from any sense of artificial reality, any intolerances of the physical body, other alien realities, foreign realities, emotional black holes, voids, corruption or interference. By letting go we fully surrender into the trust of the universe. We need to heal our juxtapositions, inner conflicts and emotional aspects such as fear, pain and insecurity to enter a state of nonduality. Self validating processing and expressing emotions will always be a factor of life, reaching a healthy flow with these communications enables life to flow. When you are in your flow, life can happen. Holding a space of love and light enables the shadow aspects to transform in to light and find expression easily. Shinning lights in to shadows allows healing, validation and acknowledgement, enabling a peaceful process in to Source and finding the Source of one's origin. Remembering under everything is infinite love and light.

What is Reality?

The question of reality goes back to the 'true nature of being human'. Reality is perception and perception is reality; we are all one, we are connected to everything, everything is us and we are everything. We can activate our reality to bring change, to create, to enable 'energies' to inspire and unite or we can excite an active process of creativity into destruction. We can release the energies that underpin us to the darkness; the void, entrapment, conflict and lack. By energising reality from a place of love, light and 'we are all one', we enable the positive side of creation to commune in love and light. We can revel in self belief in ourselves; that we are lucky, successful, popular, dependable, talented, confident, abundant and fully engaged in the world, by believing we create our world from strong foundations of trust. By holding space for each other to commune in love and light enables the shadow aspects of the self to slowly release gently and easily. Casting light on our shadows very quickly reveals the issues in light, enabling us to process and move through emotional blocks, hurdles, voids smoothly and with support.

The one area we can rely on in life to be true and to tell us truth is the 'natural' world - the natural world that is un-interfered with by man. Here we can look truth in the eye and know that what we are perceiving is real. So by working with nature, attuning to the natural world through our human technology, in love, light, understanding and dependability, we are grounded and we know we can work at building solid foundations to our development that are not interfered with in intellectual ownership, power or status. Whatever you are in the natural world, you are for real; this is the gateway into oneness.

When we step out of this we can be deluded by status, hierarchy, religion, marketing scams, political gain, academic achievement, social status, ego, economic expanse. The use of product communication for connection through these modalities of working environment are set up by society to provide a framework to prosperity, so that we may live a safe and secure life. However, at what sacrifice?

How can we remain secure in our inner self so as to embrace oneness? Trusting our own ability to allow the power of the universe to work with us and flow through us in an attuned and 'natural' manner, allows a deeper more loving and peaceful connection with people and the world around us. Moving through this process means that when our paths are aligned with others, we can move in a direction without effort so that as we work together to create newness in the world, our projects and goals arrive easily and effortlessly. This happens as divinity and the universal body of consciousness works with us and through us without any interference.

But why do we often veer away from unified consciousness? Why do we live in fear of having a happy, simple and effective life? Maybe the root to these feelings comes from the fear, that after our death, our consciousnesses could become united with a larger power without any individuality; there is a fear beyond ego in loss of 'self'. The need for individuality is an insecurity fed through the fear of the loss of identity and a loss of faith in God, Source or the Universal Body of Consciousness. On a healthy level it is the need to remain in self-love. On a spiritual level, once we have been born onto earth we also experience the same concept the other way, in the experience of being born. The trauma of losing the love of Source and God in Heaven or Nirvana when being born into a life, often comes up in a person's spiritual journey: we call it 'Individuation Trauma', the pain of disconnecting from the infinite love source. People spend their lives searching for this sensation of infinite love. When re-connecting a person to their spiritual frequency of source love, by clearing the trauma of disconnection, they are able to 'plug in to the energy' of God and Spirit and reunite with trust in the larger consciousness.

The fear of loss of self in oneness, often keeps us from embracing enlightenment. The fear of religion, fear of power, fear of knowing the truth; historically our ego can keep us limited in one framework of thought. Philosophy can provide an in-between place of understanding and question through the space of creativity. Creativity is what it is - it never needs to be proved, it can be what it needs to be and creativity can act from a place of creation as long as it is not harmful and is responsible. Creativity is therefore unrestricted and limitless in its possibilities of experience and creation. Always ask 'If I create 'this', what will the impact be?'

'The Holy Grail', the creative womb of enlightenment is considered a state of consciousness by those on the path of enlightenment. The womb is considered the place of divine creation, the female womb or the gateway into the universe of understanding, enabling the surrendering to bliss. To activate our holy grail as women, is to nurture and nourish our place of creative fertility and growth. For men, it is to hold space in the gateway to the universe, to honour and relate to creation through the engagement of the self, wisdom, sovereignty, the feminine, divine light and love, with a sensitive and embracing understanding of communications, intimacy and light-work. The energies, when fully engaged with; build, restore, nourish and expand, enabling many rewards and blissful exchanges between lovers who love truly and honour wisely. When nurturing these energies, all is possible, as the universe is embodied as the seat of creation in the lap of understanding, giving the opportunity to surrender in union to 'Divine Will' through a blissful exchange and honour of an altar of love.

Becoming Source

Source is the energy of creation, a pure white, thick energy that is infinitely wise and wholesome. At the depths of our emotional clearing, beneath the more complex layers of emotions, underneath all our complexity and debris and beyond, in peace, we reconnect with this sense of the abundant energy we name 'Source'. Every part of our energy field can be expressing itself from this position, but we put hurdles in the way, emotionally, physically and mentally. By allowing the clearing of our emotional debris through suggesting to ourselves that we align every part of our being with the infinite source light, we can emit this frequency consistently.

Traditionally through learning Reiki we are asked to channel energy from our hands, by concentrating on the Reiki symbols and by channelling the different energies to a person receiving. On an advanced level we can visualise the violet flame and become the flame, or we can become the three fold frame of Yeshua, Archangel Michael and Saint Germain: this helps to attune our inner vibration to a very far-reaching healing body. In combination with these techniques we can develop a way of working with soul-reading and emotional clearing of fear, pain and insecurity. Combining visualisations with soul rescue through visualisation and past life regression can help clearing on a deeper level. Becoming Source, allows us to send light through our beings to others and to live in light and love ourselves. Stepping in to emitting this vibration constantly allows us to regenerate energy and live in a healing vibration, so as to allow our default to find its way back to source and to relate to others through this source light.

As the Source energy embodies us we heal emotionally; all the hurdles that stop us from being at one with peace of the Source dissolve in light. We can expand this force into the heart, digestion, pelvis, root chakra, sacral centre, throat chakra, brow chakra, back up to source and become one with this infinite source of divine light. Bathing in this strength of experience allows a brilliance in that it sets the higher consciousness to create from this possibility. 'The anatomy of creation', has a meditation to help plug in.

I was feeling that all parts of myself could operate wholly if I fully connected in to the right vibration of Source consistently. I saw this as a source light of infinity; abstract pure white energy, bathing in the sacred waters, allowing sacred truth in. I felt my destiny was here, the journey was back into my own sense of beauty, of light, of Source. Releasing the forces that underpinned me, the emotions that caused me to feel unsure, I enabled the Source light to come towards me and embody me. I felt a sense of coming home. The sense that life was very much about releasing the emotional complexities again and again until eventually every part of me became Source; I could be source and let the emotional complexities fall away as I became stronger as a light being. I felt sure of myself here; there was no need to look further, this was about connecting to others who really understood their eternity, their source and were open vessels of 'creation'. From this central position of awareness I felt anything was possible. I decided to start creating my life from this position, allowing light and love to be like a waterfall through me, constantly embracing others and my sense of being. I became love emitting a strong white light that was consistently wise and resilient beyond its own know-ing. By emitting our own sense of Source we allow our vibration into the world. This ability to magnify in peace allows our presence to become sublime. Coming into my own source meant expanding my sense of presence beyond the physical like a radical beacon of light. I found the source vibration of my origin as a universal energy and I found by harnessing this frequency, I created a sense of arriving home in my experience of living and the manifestation of my dreams.

Meditation, Source

The easiest and quickest way to connect to Source is to do a meditation to 'breathe' open the chakras. By putting attention on each one, starting with the root chakra, at the base of the spine, breathing into it, opening it out, in front and behind. Then moving up to the sacral centre, then the solar plexus, the heart centre, the brow chakra, finally the crown and opening up to the divine light of source and breathing the light through the body by visualising one's breath and oxygen as light. Then to visualise a pillar of white light from a sphere of white light above the head; the white light pours from the sphere into the top of the head, moving through the centre of the human body into the earth's centre and up to the top of the sky. At the top of the sky it is important to visualise a white star light sphere similar in shape to a sun but white light. Visualise this sphere opening up at the base and connecting with the pillar of light extending from the top of your head and allow this beautiful deep peaceful energy to ooze its way down the pillar of light and into your body. It brings peace, healing, wisdom and relaxation. Allow the energy to find its way all around your body slowly breathing it through, noticing how it relaxes all your muscles and emotions. Call in the Sacred Father and Yeshua. This is the time of deliverance in trust and light.

I had a very moving experience reconnecting with the heart of God, in which I was presented with a diamond heart for protection and to deliver me in light. This spiritual understanding presents an interesting juxtaposition away from materialism but towards the diamond crystal, in protection and the sustaining of creating from and being 'source' energy. The Diamond Light Heart Energy, is presented by the Sacred Father, God and connected to from the heart, the diamond illuminates the self, strengthening one's life force, keeping a person on a high level of energetic frequency. From the Diamond Heart, we connect to different coloured diamonds in our chakras. Each one helps us to remain consistent and strong in our energy field.

Diamond Light is beyond duality; we find we can only create reality from love and light.

Diamond Light is protected by the Geodesic Dome or Metatron's cube in the aura.

Diamond Light is a grid of light energy that is global.

Diamond Light is a vibration of soul that many connect with.

Diamond Light is the diamond light energy of our hearts as presented by God.

Diamond Light allows a blessing of love and light in all activities and relationships.

Diamond Light allows an understanding through knowing and a sense of clarity in purpose.

Diamond Light restores balance, strength and harmony.

Diamond Light remains in the earth but raises us to the heavens.

Diamond Light invokes memories of wisdom and of love.

Diamond Light gives security and balance in pathways and love.

Diamond Light emits harmony, vivid complex colours and strength in all things beautiful.

Entering into the Diamond Heart and aligning to the Grid allows a journey of understanding different diamond frequencies:, all strong and purposeful energies: white diamond, black diamond, blue diamond.

Chakra Meditation, Diamond Heart Connection

To enter into our crystal diamond being, we visualise Source light coming from a heavenly position through the top of our head, bringing warm and nourishing light-energy, soothing and healing us. We allow this energy to relax every muscle in our body as we concentrate on our breathing, noticing the way the breath moves through our nose, how we feel the vacuum around our nostrils, how our lungs fill and how we find peace in the stillness of simply focusing on our breath. We visualise this breath like white light that moves through our lungs and oxygenates our blood stream. The blood cells carry this light around to every cell in our body, releasing all worry and tension. Allowing our mind to become empty, we spend time nurturing and nourishing our inner space of pure white light. As we do this we catalyse our soul to remember who we are in our truth, as a sacred child of

God. We allow this memory to bring us our sense of eternal wisdom, intimacy in love with God and in our innate being. We allow our energies to expand, through each of the chakras, starting with the root chakra in the pelvis, bringing diamond gems of knowledge and peace as we breathe into our chakra and release any blocks in front of us or behind us. We then take the energy up to the sacral under our belly button and again allow a diamond crystal to hold space, as a crystal of light, in our precious place of identity and communication. We then allow the energy to move up to our solar plexus at the base of our ribs, the place of our unfolding, we ask for a diamond crystal gem to hold a boundary in letting only pursuits that help us and serve us to relate to. We then draw our energy and attention up our heart chakra. Here we connect with Source and the Sacred Father, we allow a diamond to be presented to our soul of God, a light so bright that all those who are presented to us, will shine. We allow this strength to enable a catalyst of processes into the future, networking a diamond path of light, that has an architecture to protect us and to keep us safe. We then move with that light into our throat chakra, allowing the diamond to create a strength in our communication that enables strong development. The energy rises, filling us up with a strong and empowered sense of wisdom that satisfies our calling and enables clarity and strength in our clairvoyant vision. We allow our third eye to open, to be given the strength of third sight. We allow a letting go and a peace as we find a way through our crown chakra to our higher consciousness and gatekeeper, to enable a diamond crystal to form around the key central positions in our being. We start to see the programming of each crystal activating a path into strength that is sustainable and of light.

We realise we rise, we ascend beyond our problems, our worries and our concerns as we enter into Source: a governing light of God, which inspires our vision, our creativity and keeps us feeling the intimate support of God Love. Extending beyond our crown chakra we are able to notice a geodesic dome, which houses us in a consistent geodesic temple of diamond light. When activated and nourished this develops in to Metatron's cube, a healing grid that can be aligned with Merkaba healing.

This ignites our energies to motivate us into the pathway of diamond light as it activates the grid under our feet. As we breathe into the ground, we are able to feel the activation of light amongst the earth, demonstrating a light path of sublime existence in which the pains of resistance leave us and we are able to encounter a future outlet and development structure that is infinite in its possibilities and adjustments, allowing us to centre in to a loving space of commitment in divine understanding, that brings us home into universal understanding; into a reality that is secure, successful and safe. This reality encourages the abundance to build and the communications to inspire, as we connect to others who experience heartfelt diamond light moments of clarity, strength and bliss.

Diamonds pour out of suns that are born out of the night sky, giving light to those who navigate their pathways and gaze out into the universe with wonder in their hearts. Their true calling ignites many that bridge into God's lap of creative wisdom through the delicate celebration of the

divine embodiment to their calling. Here we see the catalysts of the stars uplift and ignite to celebrate life in their
beauty and strength of achievement. Here we see the
generous spirit of the lord, bend down to us in honour of
our spirit of prevailing illumination, as the sun multiplies
to shine forth and touch us with many blessings.

Sustaining lightness is possible when creating from
diamond light bliss, nurturing an ability to be on top of
emotions, the light of your soul, free from interference,
corruption or limit, enabled through your deliverance in
to your sovereignty and true self. The expansion of your
self in to universal presence celebrates your success in
being, in knowing and in alignment with your mission
and purpose. As these skills are nurtured so is your presence, you are deeply connected to the heart of the
universe and welcomed through a listening universe who
serves the benevolence of all. The management of living
uplifts with inspiration; a universe filled with inspiration
satisfies the adventurous heart, bringing direction, unfolding experience and love through a communicative and
collective universal consciousness.

I wish you blessings and peace as your journey unfolds,
go forth with the children of the universe to awaken and
re-vitalise your manifestation of eternal light. A light that
is consistent, dependable and strong. Blessing the days
and the minutes with a baptism of love and an endless
beauty that baths the soul in the Sacred River of Peace.

Index

Meditations

Further Reading

Below is a list of inspiring people and their books, beautiful souls with whom we are blessed to share the earth.

Soul Plan - Blue Marsden − Hay House UK 2013

Eating in to Light - Doreen Virtue − Hay House 2013

Earth Angels, a Pocket Guide - Doreen Virtue − Hay House 2014

The Lightworkers Way - Doreen Virtue − Hay House 1997

Ascended Masters and Archangels - Doreen Virtue - Hay House 2004

Talking with the Entities - Shannon O'Hara − lulu.com 2011

The Little Black Book of Relationships − Dr. Kacie Crisp − Createspace 2011

Journey of Souls and Destiny of Souls - Dr Michael Newton − Llewellyn 1994 U.S.

The Business of Creativity - Michael Jacobson − Harriman House 2013

There is no Business Like Soul Business - Derek Rydall − Michael Wiese Productions 2007

The Law of Emergence - Derek Rydall − Atria Books/Beyond Words 2015

Silent Pain - Helen Germanos (Chronic Fatigue Therapy) − Troubador Publishing 2015

The Magi - Diane Pegler, Meditations of the Diamond Light Grid − Balbao Press 2013

Art - articles www.artlyst.com Editor - Paul Carter Robinson

The Serpent Grail - The Truth Behind the Holy Grail, The Philosophers Stone and the Elixir of Life - Philip Gardiner and Gary Osborn − Watkins 2006

The Journey - Brandon Bay − Atria Books 2012

Apologies to the Divine Female, Apologies to the Divine Masculine are articles on the internet, further writing by Jeff Brown

Wheels of Light; Rosalyn L. Bruyere published by Simon & Schuster Ltd 1994

You Can Heal Your Life - Louise Hay, Hay House 1984

Please note that the websites and information listed may change and be different. Creative Development Therapy - www.belovedlight.com

Easily accessible Healing/Nurture/Self-Management Tools

Access Consciousness - Dain Heer, Gary Douglas, Kacie Crisp, Talking with the Entities - Shannon O'Hara

Guided Self-Healing - Dr Andrew H. Hahn and Kathy Eckles

Soul Contract Planning - Blue Marsden

Hypnotherapy

Emotional Freedom Technique

Questions for Coaches

Kinesiology

Reiki

G.R.O.W. model of development

Gratitude

The universe comes together in infinite ways. I am blessed to have received much love, healing and support from many, so much so that I can share the process of logos and omnipresence with others:

My beloved, family and friends whom have walked with me.

Thank you also to my intuitive development groups, themselves therapists, whom supported and inspired me to share my journey and processes of healing as I wrote 'A Life of Bliss', especially Annie Geyde, Valerie Stoner, Michelle Shrimp and Terri Charles.

Phil Braiden whom tirelessly worked with me in trance and hypnotherapy to help me explore and navigate my soul.

The proof readers Michelle Shrimp and Colleen French who have done their best to enable a flowing read.

Annalisa Cattani and her family; whom opened their homes and shared their lives with me in creative and inspirational living.

Svetlana Danton-Rees and her family for giving me the use of a log cabin and a hot tub in the Cambrian Mountains - Wales www.oakwoodlodges.co.uk. Thank you for so much energetic recharge and an environment to write from which put me in my Bliss.

My clients, this is for all for you.

Blessed be

Printed in Great Britain
by Amazon